Also by Paul Rezendes

TRACKING & THE ART OF SEEING:
HOW TO READ ANIMAL TRACKS AND SIGN

With Paulette Roy

WETLANDS: THE WEB OF LIFE

PAUL REZENDES

JEREMY P. TARCHER / PUTNAM

a member of

PENGUIN PUTNAM INC.

New York

THE
WILD
WITHIN

Adventures in Nature and

Animal Teachings

73746

Outdoor recreational activities are by their very nature potentially hazardous. All participants in such activities must assume the responsibility for their own actions and safety. If you have any health problems or medical conditions, consult with your physician before undertaking any outdoor activities.

Most Tarcher/Putnam books are available at special quantity discounts for bulk purchases for sales promotions, premiums, fund-raising, and educational needs. Special books or book excerpts also can be created to fit specific needs. For details, write Putnam Special Markets, 375 Hudson Street, New York, NY 10014.

Jeremy P. Tarcher/Putnam
a member of
Penguin Putnam Inc.
375 Hudson Street
New York, NY 10014
www.penguinputnam.com

Library of Congress Cataloging-in-Publication Data

Rezendes, Paul.
The wild within: adventures in nature and animal teachings / by Paul Rezendes.
p.   cm.
ISBN 0-87477-931-6 (alk. paper)
1. Natural history.   2. Tracking and trailing.   3. Nature—Psychological aspects.   I. Title.
QH45.5.R495   1998   98-11725 CIP
508—dc21

Printed in the United States of America

1   3   5   7   9   10   8   6   4   2

This book is printed on acid-free paper. ∞

Book design by Jennifer Ann Daddio
Interior photographs © 1998 by Paul Rezendes

1/99
Ing.

ACKNOWLEDGMENTS

Many thanks to all the people who have contributed so generously and graciously to the creation of this book. In particular, I'd like to thank, first and foremost, my collaborator, Kenneth Wapner, for his dedication, hard work, and creative contributions to the text. I especially value the gift of his friendship and his flexibility and perseverance through the challenges of our joint writing process.

A big thank-you to my editor at Jeremy P. Tarcher, Wendy Hubbert, for her bursting enthusiasm for the book from the outset and for her meticulous care in making sure we got things right; to my agents, Gail Ross and Howard Yoon, for connecting me with Tarcher, for their sound advice, and for their patience with my lack of publishing-world savvy.

To my friend Dr. Ray Amore, Ph.D., who many years ago pointed me in the right direction, a special thanks for his invaluable assistance in refining some of the philosophical points of the text and for reviewing the manuscript.

Thanks to Gary Chassman at Verve Editions for his help in the early stages of the project, Pat Styer for help with research, Susan Davis for transcriptions, Bill Fournier, Bill Byrne, and Lisa Bertoldi for reviewing the draft manuscripts, Marie Lehman for administrative assistance, and Mary Ellen Scribner, my office manager, for her very capable handling of whatever came her way and for her calm demeanor in the midst of a hundred pressing deadlines.

Thanks also to my tracking apprentices and to the many tracking students through the last dozen-plus years for being my teachers.

Last, I thank my wife, Paulette, whose invisible contributions to this book and most important, to my life, are the greatest of all.

To my children,
Kevin, Paula, and Lianna

CONTENTS

Foreword   *1*

Introduction   *3*

1. THE WEB OF LIFE   7

2. WRESTLING THE BEAR   25

3. LOONS AND THE LESSONS OF LOVE   49

4. STALKING SILENCE   69

5. THE TERRITORY OF SELF   97

6. SHARING THE PATH   119

7. SPEAKING WITHOUT WORDS   141

8. THE DANCE OF LIFE AND DEATH   161

9. COYOTE INTELLIGENCE   185

10. THE WILD WITHIN   199

Permissions   *219*

FOREWORD

This is a truly remarkable book, and therefore I'm in the odd position for a foreword writer of not wanting to say too much about it in advance—I don't want to draw for you the many conclusions that formed in my own mind as I read it, for it should be a rich, and somewhat nerve-wracking, adventure for all who read it.

Paul Rezendes writes with authority about his intense degradation as leader of a motorcycle gang, a literal Devil's Disciple. He writes with equal authority about his intense self-examination as an adept of various yogic sects. And finally he writes with truly unusual power about his—well, in some sense, about *dissolving* his self into the world of nature.

A magnificently accomplished animal tracker, it is almost as if he follows the trails of hare and bobcat and coyote into some other realm, not into some Carlos Castaneda *Other World,* but simply into the actual physical universe that is our home. We rarely inhabit it, of course—probably most of us get through entire lifetimes with little more than a glimpse of it, since we are so firmly located in the various mental constructions Rezendes describes so well. But I could imagine this book serving as a sort of field guide for those who are intrepid and modest enough to make the trip.

In describing his journey he manages to provide a deep answer to what may be the single great problem of our age. Though, as gurus back to the Buddha have pointed out, we have always been inclined to self-centeredness, we now live in a consumer society that has made a great virtue of that curse. We are supposed to locate ourselves at the center of the world—each of us is supposed to regard ourself as the one great blessed core of existence. Breaking out of that trance is damnably hard, especially when we're rehypnotized each day by all the wiles of all the marketers and pitchmen. But somehow—and this underlies almost all great nature writing—contact with the physical world, what David Abram has called the "more-than-human" world, can be the bracing slap in the face that helps restore us to our senses. Rezendes captures this notion of wildness about as well as it can be captured in words, and, what is better, he provides some clues for how to find it out for ourselves.

I cannot imagine anyone dismissing this book, though it deals tangentially with subjects like Eastern philosophy that Americans are notoriously allergic to. The volume simply rings with too much integrity to be taken any way but seriously. Rezendes started tracking bobcats, and ended up tracking himself, and in so doing he has laid out a trail for others to follow. Use caution, go slowly—but go.

BILL MCKIBBEN

INTRODUCTION

For more than a decade I've been taking people from all walks of life into the woods to learn how to read animal track and sign. Many of my tracking students live in cities and don't often come into contact with nature, but I think they come to my workshops because they feel that intimacy with nature is essential to their lives.

Over the years, I've become convinced, by observing my workshop students and through my own experience as a tracker, that there is no better way to connect with nature than by learning how to read track and sign. But, for me, there has been something missing in these workshops. We really can't understand nature until we understand ourselves—and so this book begins where my classes leave off. It is filled with the adventures in nature that have illuminated my inward journey—adventures that have taught me about fear, life and death, aggression, compassion, direct communication, silence, the true nature of intelligence, and love. The book also contains exercises that can be done in the woods, a city park, or a backyard. These exercises are designed to redirect our attention from the chatter in our minds, the pressures of work, our troublesome relationships, and the mundane details that consume our lives. They offer an opportunity for us to awaken to our surroundings, and I hope they help you understand the connection between the world around us and our interior "landscape."

In the book, I have drawn from episodes in my own life. Through retracing the tracks that led me to become a tracker, I arrived at realizations about nature and the self. It is a journey that hasn't always been easy.

In the early 1960s, I was the leader of two notorious motorcycle gangs. I led a violent, criminal life. I dealt drugs and I participated in events that now seem to belong to another life, another person. Busted for possession of drugs and an illegal weapon, I was sentenced to five to ten years in prison. Fortunately, I did not serve time. But my bust was a wake-up call, propelling me on a search for truth. I tried to be a good Catholic but soon became disillusioned with that path. I practiced hatha yoga and eventually became a yoga teacher. I studied the work of Krishnamurti intensely, and founded and led an ashram in southeastern Massachusetts.

It wasn't until 1980 that I began to synthesize this spiritual work with my work as a tracker. As a child, I had learned about nature from my mother, my first teacher in the language of the forest. She would take me into the woods near our home in southeastern Massachusetts and teach me the names of plants and which ones were good to eat. She helped me become sensitive to all living creatures. The forest behind our house became the scene of many of my childhood adventures, but also the setting for the beginning of my spiritual search. It was a place where I felt the wonder of creation and started questioning what my place was in all this beauty.

In later life, when I'd pick up the trail of an animal in the snow on a crisp cold winter day and follow it off into the woods, it was like starting an adventure. I was trying to learn about the animal in the same way that my mother had taught me to experience nature when I was a child, and I let the animal guide me. I learned to discern the way it was moving based on its tracks. Without seeing the creature itself, I could tell if it had been walking, trotting, loping, galloping, or looking to the left or right. I learned where animals ate, where they slept, what their scat looked like, and even what it smelled like. I learned how animals hunt, what they eat, when and where to find them, how to get close to them, and how to move silently through the forest and see animals before they see you.

But all the while, tracking was for me more than scent posts, scat diameters, and middens: it was a potent tool for learning about myself. As I became intimate with the language of the forest, I came to see that the world of nature and my own mind were inextricably linked. Nature inspired me to spend a lifetime asking the deep questions that are at the heart of this book: What is thought? Where does the self end and the world begin? What is truth? What gives meaning to our lives?

Ultimately, we must each answer such questions for ourselves. Tracking is one way to begin the exploration. This book reflects my path and my search. In it you will read about bears, bobcats, moose, foxes, and many other creatures of the forest. And you will read about the cunning ways of a devious animal called self.

1.

THE WEB
OF LIFE

TRACKING BOBCAT CAN BE HELL. THEY JUST LOVE TO take you through the thickest possible terrain, like the hillside smothered in mountain laurel across which I was leading eight students that had signed up for my predator tracking program. On our hands and knees, we pushed our snowshoes ahead of us, our day packs snarled in the laurel's twisted branches. Twigs scraped our faces. I pointed out to the group that the even spacing of the tracks in front of us indicated that the bobcat, low to the ground and lithe, had moved effortlessly through the thickets.

My students and I were getting to know this bobcat, learning how it hunted, where it liked to lay up, where it deposited its scent, how it moved through its territory. This was the cat's domain, heavy cover, perfectly suited to its slinking, secretive nature. We were learning that there is no better way to get to know an animal than to track it; but we were also learning that tracking, and knowing, are often hard work. My students had been grumbling behind me; every so often someone emitted a stifled curse.

Snow cascaded from the laurel tops down our napes and backs. We penetrated deeper into the laurel, and I felt the group become quiet and attentive. It was as if the ghost of the cat was out in front of us. We began to move like the bobcat, see like the bobcat. Its tracks were our tracks, its world, our world. We had found our inner bobcat! A part of ourselves that had been there all along. What a little suffering will do, I thought.

I've told my students that we don't expect to track the bobcat down. That's not the kind of tracking that I teach or practice. Tracking for me is not about the clichéd images of a hunter stalking a buck, or a Native American in a Western movie tracking a villain, troops following behind. For me, tracking is an educational process that opens the door to an animal's life—and to our own.

As my students and I moved deep into the laurel, I became wary. I had once found a bobcat den in exactly this kind of country, on the side of a steep hill, deep in laurel. I didn't want to intrude on another den site, especially with a big group—the cat might abandon the den. Bobcats usually don't den when they're done hunting. Instead they have lays throughout their territory. The lays are like motel rooms. They go from one to another—one day here, one day there (these cats are nocturnal). Or they may stay in a favorite lay three days running.

My students followed me onto the face of a wide spur that jutted from the hillside. We were approaching a steep incline scored by ledges. I sensed our bobcat was heading for those ledges, where it had a lay, and, sure enough, the cat led us out along shelves of rock, slick with ice and snow.

I cautioned my students to take care, to keep themselves mindful and in the present, to take the journey along the ledges step by careful step. The ledges were very slippery. The drop-off on our left is about twenty feet straight down to jagged rock outcroppings and a steep slope of snow-covered scree. The rock wall on our right bellied out. We had to squeeze along it, making ourselves thin and flat, feeling the rock up against our shoulders and knees, pressing cold and hard against our faces, pushing us out toward the edge.

The cat's tracks padded blithely ahead. I almost called everything off and turned the group around when the ledges opened a bit and we had room to breathe. But I still kept the group tight behind me and *en garde*, because of the drop and the icy patches on the path. We came to a place of beautiful little semi-caves scooped out of the cliff face. Shelves of stone overhung these little snow-free cubbies. The bobcat had checked each one, until it came to a particularly attractive cubby carpeted with dead leaves. In the leaves was a small, matted impression where the cat had rested. It was a hard-to-approach, snug, hidden spot.

I've found more bobcat lays than I can remember, and almost every one had a scenic view. This one was no exception. It looked south, out over the rolling hills and dense woodlands. In the distance, I could see water. We were in northcentral Massachusetts, on the protected lands around Quabbin Reservoir, one of the wildest places in southern New England. There were no houses in sight. No sound of traffic. Only the moan of the wind.

We stood there, taking in the view, looking at the lay, all of us feeling very close to that cat and exhilarated that it had led us to one of its secret places. After our hard morning tracking, we had a sense of completion and closure, as though we had come to the end of a journey.

But the bobcat wasn't through with us yet. Its tracks led from the cubby along the ledges to where the ledges broke and the hillside sloped steep and slippery downward. The slope was snow-covered, and under the snow I knew were loose wet leaves, slick as banana peels, and shifting scree.

In my tracking workshops I usually have a rule that we don't disturb an animal's tracks. I like to leave them as pristine as possible. I want to make sure everyone in the group has the chance to read what's written in the tracks. But I also don't want to interfere because to me tracks are an animal's signature, a way in which it communicates to the world, an essential and dramatic part of the environment.

With our clumsy human movements, our whole day, so far, had disturbed the bobcat's trail. It was impossible not to muck up the tracks through the laurels and on the ledges. And now it was impossible to get down the hillside without sending rocks avalanching in front of us, half standing, half sitting, making a racket, coming to the base of the scree and brushing each other off. We looked horrified at the slope that the bobcat had descended without disturbing a leaf. Now it looked like a herd of buffalo had stampeded down its side.

The cat continued to move down, down, down through the hardwood forest of beech, oak, and ash toward lowland marshes, wet meadows, shrub swamps, and bogs. This is typical. Bobcats will lay up in the highlands and hunt in the wetlands. The cat moved toward the shrub swamp but then veered westward. Had I been wrong about where it was going?

Behind me, a student asked why the cat had changed direction. From long experience tracking, I've found that it's better to wait and see, not to force explanations. Often my students are too anxious for answers. I tell them to be patient, to let the animals tell you about their lives.

The cat took us into an area of forest where young hemlock saplings had sprung up close together, their limbs almost interlocked. It was a dense, sheltered place, scruffy and remote. We picked our way through, slowly and carefully, pushing back branches, ducking low, shielding our eyes with our arms. We broke out into an opening.

Big hemlocks towered overhead, dimming the winter light. The snow in front of us was blotched red and yellow from the spilled body fluids of a dead deer. Pieces of the deer's carcass were scattered about, its hair strewn in a twelve-foot radius. Half a leg, the spinal column, and the head with some hide clinging to it were all that remained, except for the deer's rumen (the stomach contents), which few animals will eat. The snow in front of us was completely matted with tracks of various animals—coyotes, fishers, and domestic dogs.

The group was shaken. Some of them turned away while others looked on, unable to take their eyes off the carcass. One student asked me what happened. They all fell silent, waiting for the reply. I glimpsed tears in one student's eyes, expressing the raw emotion that such a scene can evoke.

"Let's see if we can piece it together," I said. "A scene like this can be hard to take. But perhaps when we come to an understanding of exactly what went on here, you may respond to it in a different way."

"Who killed the deer?" someone asked.

"There's no way to know that," I said. "The deer died here about two days ago, maybe less."

"Come on! There's hardly anything left!"

"Things can happen very quickly at a kill site. There have been many animals feeding here. Let me paint as full a picture as I can of what has happened here. To begin with, this deer, in essence, has grown up not only in the forest but *from* the forest." I saw I was getting blank stares, so I tried to explain. "When it was born it weighed only four to eight pounds. When it died, I would guess it probably weighed in just over 100 pounds, a young adult. It doesn't look like it was very big."

They stood there, next to the kill, taking it in. I explained that the deer was able to grow, gain mass, by feasting on acorns in the fall, putting on as much fat as it could to carry it through the winter. During the winter months, it browsed on hemlock, juniper, dogwood, viburnum, maple, oak, witch hazel, and many other types of woody plants and fungi. In summer, it gorged itself on all kinds of herbaceous plants and leaves, including some of its preferred foods, like jewelweed, wild lettuce, and dogwood leaves.

That organic mass contained in the trees and shrubs, in the light, air, water, soil, and microbes, is the living forest. The deer had, literally, materialized from *this*. The deer *was* the forest breathing, walking, mating, living, and dying.

The organic mass of the deer had come from thousands of elements, from all directions in the forest, to this one point at the kill site. Now it was returning to the forest in every direction through the animals feeding on the carcass. Our bobcat had come to the deer and taken a few scraps. Coyote, fisher, weasel, fox, raven, crow, even the chickadees flitting from branch to branch, had fed on the carcass.

It was evident to our scientific minds, looking at the kill site in this way, that on a fundamental level the deer was the forest and the forest was the deer—both were inextricably part of the web of life. But the deer's carcass also exposed another facet of the web of life that was difficult for our intellects to grasp. There are some aspects of life that thought cannot understand. Thought works by compartmentalizing, creating boundaries—dividing the whole into parts. In order to fully comprehend the meaning before us, we had to go beyond thought.

The deer's death had changed the direction of the bobcat that we had been following—not only the direction in which it was traveling, but its whole life. When a bobcat hunts, timing is critical. When and where the cat is in relation to its prey often determines whether the prey dies or the bobcat eats and lives. Whatever happens to the bobcat at a given moment changes everything else for the rest of the bobcat's life. The vast matrix of timing that affected the movement of the deer had affected the movement of the bobcat, too. Because the deer had died, the bobcat had veered from its path to the marsh and we had also veered.

Seen in this light, it becomes clear that no movement on this planet is separate from any other movement. The planet moves as a whole. We, too, are part of this movement. What happened at that kill site and the path the bobcat was traveling were the same movement as all of us tracking, walking, living, and dying.

One of my students seemed to want to say something, so I nodded in her direction. "You seem to be talking about two different things," she said. "First you were talking about organic mass, the interconnections between the microbes in the soil, the deer, the trees, and other animals. Then you started to talk about timing and movement. I'm not sure I understand the connection."

"It's tricky," I said. "In nature there is just the movement of the present. All organic exchanges are that movement. They are in flux, all happening together in the *now*. Thought divides that movement up into past, present, and future, thus creating the idea of time. But the past and the future are happening in the present. If you can see it that way, you can understand that the organic interconnectedness of the elements is not static. The mix is constantly changing. Who we are now is all that has happened before us, happening as us, in the now. Who we are moves us into the next moment and the next. All our ancestors and everything they did, every decision they made, everything they learned is happening now. And our ancestors are not only people—but also the river, mountain, rock, fire, land, ocean, forest, bobcat, and deer."

We can say that it takes an hour to go from point A to point B, but that whole hour is in the moment, and each moment is constantly changing. Sometimes we try to stop the movement, because we are afraid of change, the unknown, and death. The movement of life, however, is constantly bringing us into the unknown. This is why it can be so hard for us to be really present, to be in the moment, in the now. We're afraid to be. So we escape into the past, our memory of what happened, which doesn't seem to be changing. It is static, safe. We cling to it. But by doing so we make ourselves into static beings, which puts us into constant conflict with the ever-changing movement of life.

Trees, stones, earth, deer bones, bobcat are constantly changing form, one into the other. You might say all these elements constitute movement over time. They are not really static *objects* if they are constantly changing. This kill site was an example of change. The fact that it represented change was why many of my students have found it disturbing.

We are used to seeing things as living or dead, existing or not existing. A deer is a deer, not a bobcat. We see things as separate, but we need to explore wholeness. We need to understand what keeps us from embracing all of life, which includes death. We need to journey into the totality of who we are, into the web of life that connects us to all things in an eternal present.

My students and I left the kill site and picked up the bobcat's tracks on the perimeter of the track-matted snow. The cat continued on its way to the lowlands, into the swamp. It had taken us through laurel thickets, along slippery ledges and down the face of cliffs. Now it was leading us into the swamp, an environment with its own challenges and perils.

The swamps were frozen, and tracking through them was a tricky business. The snow cover made the thickness of the ice we walked on impossible to gauge. I tuned my ears, listening for the sound of running water, which meant thin ice. In the past, I'd seen the person right next to me fall through thin ice, while beneath my feet the ice was thick. The water in the swamp was probably shallow, but you never know. There are places where the water is deep. If one of my students got soaked, hypothermia was a real possibility. I told them to follow in my steps. If I didn't fall in, most likely they wouldn't.

Many types of animals are part of the shrub swamp ecosystem—frogs, salamanders, snakes, mice, voles, wood ducks, beaver, bears, and bobcat. Not one creature in the swamp escapes being affected by a single leaf that falls. As a fallen leaf begins to decompose, it is fed on by zooplankton, tiny microscopic animals and their larvae. The zooplankton, in turn, are consumed by immature fish and the larvae of predatory insects, which themselves are food for amphibians, reptiles, larger fish, and birds, all the way up the food chain to our bobcat. Shrubs such as viburnums and highbush blueberry, which attract feeding snowshoe hares to the swamp in winter, pick up nutrients from the decomposing leaves and zooplankton. The falling leaf, the blueberries in summer, darting minnows—all are part of the trail of our bobcat.

Although the going was rough, there was no way we were going to give up the cat. I could tell by its trail that it was beginning to hunt. An excited student asked me what in its tracks indicated this. I pointed to snowshoe hare sign, low branches of shrubbery nipped to a forty-five-degree angle. Browsing hare often leave this angular bite:

a snip, sharp and clean. Deer browse tends to be blunt, horizontal. I reminded the group that we had seen no deviation in the cat's tracks when it crossed the trails of squirrel and deer. From that I deduced that the cat wasn't in a hunting mode at that moment but was headed for hunting grounds. Now, in hare country, we could see by the cat's tracks that it was checking each nook and cranny of every stump and hollow. All the while the snowshoe hare sign kept increasing.

The cat brought us into thick highbush blueberry. I scanned the terrain. "We're in for it, again!" I remarked to the group.

They were good-humored about it, fortunately. Everybody removed their snowshoes. We pushed through the wiry blueberry branches on our hands and knees as the bobcat wended its way through the lowlands. Hare runs are like little highways, and by the side of the most heavily traveled run this cat picked a spot to sit and wait. This is often how bobcats hunt. A bobcat's sitting place in the snow shows the cat turning in one spot as if it were on an axis; its front paw prints face outward in the circle that it has made. I try to take a lesson from bobcats. If we could sit like they do, for hours, with the kind of attention they use as they wait for prey, we would discover much about ourselves.

With great cunning, the cat had picked a place where a downed tree blocked the hares' run. The tree trunk was close to the ground, but with enough room for a hare to squeeze underneath. Well-worn tracks told us that this is just what the hares had been doing. The cat had hidden itself behind a stump just past the fallen tree, so it wouldn't be seen by a snowshoe hare coming down the run until the hare ducked under the tree, came out the other side, and was face-to-face with the cat. This looked like a guaranteed meal. It was amazing that the bobcat had picked such a strategic place to position itself.

We investigated further. A story was written there in the snow. We saw that the hare came along the path, but not from the bobcat's right, under the tree, but from the bobcat's left, where the cat had no cover. The hare spotted the cat. Its tracks indicated a quick turn, and the chase was on!

Tracks told of tremendous leaps and zigzag scurries. The hare streaked one way, then another, trying to throw the cat off. The cat pursued, at first making short thirty-eight-inch leaps, then astounding ninety-three-inch leaps! There was incredible pressure in the tracks where both animals landed. Snow was thrown for quite a distance. The bobcat chased the snowshoe hare for about one hundred yards, then gave up.

We were exhilarated to see all this played out for us in the snow. We'd seen a graphic example of survival in the animal world. This time, the hare had escaped. Next time, who knows? In tracking the bobcat we'd become intimate with its world and its life, and most important, we'd come to see that its life and world were not separate from our own.

In order to embrace the web of life yourself, try tracking an animal. You don't have to go to some exotic place. You don't have to track a bobcat, a mountain lion, or a wolf. You can track in your own backyard, in little pockets of woodland, in suburbia, or even in a city park. It doesn't matter what kind of animal you track.

A fascinating exercise is to track your house cat. You could actually start indoors. After all, tracking is observation. It is learning about an animal through observing its movements via its tracks and trail patterns. If you could follow a wild animal, watching its every movement without disturbing its natural behavior, that would be by far the best kind of tracking. With a wild animal, that's next to impossible. But with your house cat, you might be able to pull it off.

The trick is to watch your cat without the cat being aware that you're observing it. One interesting behavior a house cat might exhibit is pointing its rear to an object like a table leg. Its tail will be up and quivering. This is what a bobcat does when it urinates on an object to mark its territory. Note where your cat places its feet when it exhibits this marking behavior. If you follow your cat's tracks outside in the snow, mud, or sand, you can get a clue by the placement of the tracks as to whether your cat is marking its territory.

Observe your cat outside, anywhere near your home where it leaves tracks. Watch the cat as it walks, trots, runs, or bounds. Note the behavior first, then examine the different tracks and trails the animal leaves. Through persistent observation, you'll learn what track patterns are associated with each gait. Eventually, you'll be able to figure out your cat's gaits just through the track and trail patterns.

You'll be amazed as you uncover your cat's world. See how far it roams outside. See how many animals it kills—birds, shrews, voles, mice. Perhaps your cat's tracks will meet up with those of a red fox. Maybe your cat has made friends with it! That's been known to happen.

Try tracking a rabbit as it seeks out food in a suburban area. Find out what the rabbit eats. Find its form (nest) and where it has its young. Track a white-footed mouse. The mouse may reveal secret entrances to your house, putting an end to a lot of problems. You can track a raccoon at the water's edge in a city park. You'll be surprised to find them there. I've actually seen raccoon tracks in an alley in the Bronx, deep in New York City.

The day moved toward evening, but I could still see the sun through a film of clouds. Dead trees with stumpy branches, shorn of bark, poked into a steely sky. My students were cold, and I wanted to get them moving again. We picked up the bobcat's tracks where it stopped chasing the hare. The cat moved to the swamp's edge, where the ice was thin, almost wispy, cracking and crinkling beneath our feet. I was relieved to see that the cat moved off the ice into a lowland forest of conifers. It had picked up another cat's trail, and it walked in the first cat's tracks. We followed the two cats through the forest. They picked up an old stone wall and walked along its top for two hundred yards, then they jumped off and began moving uphill.

We noticed that both cats seemed to go out of their way to inspect an old, soft, punky stump. One or both of them urinated on it. The second animal stepped so precisely in the other's tracks that it was hard to tell which animal was urinating. The tracks revealed that one or both cats had backed up to the stump and squirted backward onto it. The cats then left in the direction that they faced when they urinated. As trackers, our group didn't take things like this for granted. Each piece of information brought us closer to the life of the animal.

Knowing the bobcat's direction was crucial information when we next tried to track the animal without the aid of its tracks. Amazing as it sounds, it's possible to track bobcats with your nose. Following the bobcat through the day, we had seen that it urinated frequently. And even with just this one day tracking, my students had learned that there are certain objects that cats prefer to mark with their urine. Especially here in the woods of New England, cats gravitate to soft, punky stumps, like dogs to fire hydrants, perhaps choosing them because they absorb urine and scent.

Cats will also urinate on the underside of a leaning tree. This may protect their scent from weather. They will mound leaves, small piles three to four inches high and around six and one half inches in diameter. These seem to be made specifically as urine repositories and are almost always located under rock overhangs. Bobcats are inclined to urinate at the edges of these rock overhangs, usually when they are leaving an area. These scent markings are clues to the direction in which the bobcat is moving.

The more time you spend tracking bobcat, the easier it becomes to pick out bobcat scenting objects. Knowing the direction in which the cat is going will guide you to the next scent mark. Eventually, you won't need tracks to follow a bobcat or know whether it's in a certain area. All you'll need is your sniffer.

After it scented the punky old stump, our bobcat followed the other bobcat through the woods. Both cats liked to walk along narrow logs whenever they got a chance. They took to these logs like high-wire artists, catwalking along their narrow rounded tops as if to show off their balance and poise.

Eventually, our bobcat veered off the other one's trail. We could tell it was our cat because its tracks were fresher, vividly incised in the snow. We came to a small clearing where our bobcat seemed to walk right up to a gray squirrel, and the gray squirrel seemed to hop right up to the bobcat, giving itself to the predator's jaws. There was no evidence in the squirrel's trail of any effort to bound out of the bobcat's way. The cat hadn't even broken stride. There was a round circular area in the snow where the cat had put the squirrel down and eaten it. Nothing but a little fur, specks of blood, and the tip of the squirrel's tail remained.

The group stood in a tight circle, silently looking at the kill site. We all sensed that in this clearing something of great importance had happened. After our day of tracking, after all the time we had put in becoming intimate with the bobcat's movements, the squirrel offering itself to the bobcat's jaws was not something that was just happening "out there," in a world separate from us and our concerns. It was an event that was happening to us as well.

I told my students that to become intimate with the outer landscape it is important to become intimate with the inner landscape. The two are not separate. The inner landscape is as vast, deep, and wild as the outer landscape—and the path into the inner landscape is a path less traveled. The path into the outer landscape is well-worn and well-explored. We can scientifically grasp the connections between all living things. We can empirically prove the web of life. But the path into the inner landscape is obscure and difficult. There is an animal there. It's a domesticated animal that is cunning, calculating, and very shrewd. It is full of secrecy and fear. It hides its tracks. That animal is the self, the thinker of the thoughts, the feeler of the feelings.

The light was draining from the clearing where the squirrel's track had come to an abrupt end in the snow. The forest was clothed in shades of gray. I knew we would soon retreat to the warmth and safety of our cars and homes, the human environment of food and talk and laughter. The bobcat would rouse itself from its lay in a bed of leaves. As the stars poked through the hardwoods and the temperature dropped, the bobcat would start hunting, moving over the land, down into the swamps, its eyes bright and its tracks silent.

I asked my students to embark on another, perhaps even more

fascinating adventure—to track the self. Track it like we tracked the bobcat. Figuratively, there would be snow falling down our backs, branches scraping our faces. We might tumble off cliffs or into the tangled swamps of thought. There are lots of things inside us that we might not want to discover, encounters we might not want to have, things we might not want to see. But we would learn much about ourselves: who we really are, and our place in the web of life.

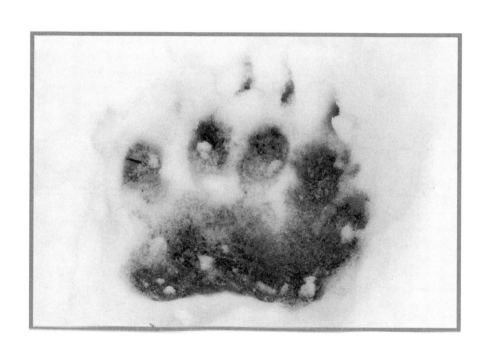

2.

WRESTLING
THE BEAR

MY WIFE, PAULETTE, AND I DIDN'T REALIZE WHAT A blisteringly hot day it was until we stepped from our air-conditioned car. The heat took our breath away—a still, sodden, choking heat. Voracious blackflies swarmed every inch of bare skin, crawling up our sleeves and under our collars. Horse flies left burning welts. We scrambled for head nets and bug spray. Even so, we were both badly bitten and drenched in sweat by the time we had unstrapped the canoe from the roof of the car, unpacked our gear, and started paddling up the Oswegatchie River in the Adirondack Mountains of upstate New York.

Out on the water the bugs should have been better, but they weren't. We had a mile to go to our rendezvous point with our friends from *Wild Earth,* a cutting-edge environmental magazine. They were going to guide us into the Five Ponds Wilderness, one of the largest remaining swaths of old growth forest east of the Mississippi, where I planned to take photographs for a book I was working on.

Bugs ate us alive in the stifling heat, and a cautionary voice inside me said, *Go back, fool, trouble waits.* But I told myself that Paulette and I were outdoor educators. Bugs and heat were our stock-in-trade.

Besides, I was leery of feelings of self-pity and despair. We humans are programmed to crave comfort and pleasure. We fear discomfort and avoid it like the plague. Well, I wasn't going to avoid it. I had work to do.

Sitting in the stern of the canoe I noticed how the blackflies burrowed under the elastic edges of Paulette's head net, feasting on the soft meat of her neck and ears. She was bleeding from numerous bites by the time we arrived at the rendezvous campsite and had developed a migraine headache. She sat with her head in her hands, helpless, as I unloaded the canoe and set up camp. She crawled inside our tent, curled into a fetal position, and rested in the sweltering heat while I braved the bugs and photographed the river and the surrounding country.

Our camp was on an upland site, looking out over the Oswegatchie and its sprawling wetlands of thick water-loving shrubs. At one end of camp, boulders dropped steeply to the river's edge. From the bluff's crest there was a magnificent westerly view of low marsh and forest through which the river snaked.

While I was photographing I kept thinking, *Soon it will be evening and the blackflies will disappear.* Finally, the sun dropped behind the low mountains. On cue, the blackflies vanished. No sooner had they gone when out came the mosquitoes, with a vengeance. They were ravenous! I checked on Paulette. She still couldn't move, so I dipped a washcloth in the cool water of the river and placed it on her forehead. I hoped that this would lessen the pounding in her head, but it didn't appear to have any immediate effect.

I ate a hurried dinner with the rest of the group. We stood around a smoke fire, eyes screwed tight, bitter fumes searing our throats. And the voice in my head was back, saying, *Go home, fools, trouble waits!*

The mosquitoes soon drove us to our tents. Some of our party had yet to arrive, and during the night Paulette and I heard them coming into camp, swearing, sobbing, slapping at the bugs. We heard them ripping off clothes and hurling themselves into the river.

The next morning everyone looked horrible, swollen and bleeding.

"This is ridiculous!" said John Davis, at the time the editor of *Wild Earth* and a veteran outdoorsman. "I've had it. If you want to go into the old growth, I'll show you where it is on the map, but I'm out of here!"

Our other friends (all seven of them!) followed suit. Paulette, too, was inclined to leave. But she said it was my decision. I sniffed the air, pretending that I was thinking, although I already knew what my decision would be. A slight breeze was rustling the treetops, and the bugs did not seem quite so bad.

"We'll stay," I told Paulette.

"Well, I guess we might as well give it a try," she said.

What a trooper! She later told me that under these game words she was thinking, *Why am I married to the only guy who wants to go upriver into the bush when everybody else is heading for home?*

Since our arrival the day before, canoes had been heading out of the bush. Davis and crew were not the only ones opting for security and comfort. I had a strong premonition as we watched them go that Paulette and I were heading off into deep wilderness alone.

It was still early when we pushed off, but it was already hot. The sun blazed in the sky. The river was slow moving, twenty-five to thirty feet wide. In places it narrowed, winding and turning back on itself through flat scrubby shrub swamps—an airless place, hot and tight. We bent our backs against the current and kept having to pull and pry on the turns. Occasionally, the river opened to vistas of balsam fir, pine, and spruce. Then the banks would close, and we'd be burrowing through a labyrinth of sedges, meadowsweet, alder, and highbush blueberry.

Beaver burrows pocked the riverbank. We spotted muskrat droppings and otter tracks. Kingfishers spun over the marsh. A great blue heron took flight at our approach, its deep croaks carrying over forest and swamp. Delicate purple flutes of wild iris nestled in vigorous cords of grass.

The breeze picked up as we pulled into camp that afternoon, cutting the heat and blowing away at least some of the bugs. The camp was lovely. It sat atop a bluff over steep rapids that tumbled between big boulders, emptying into a pool thirty feet in diameter. On the right side of the pool was a grassy swath. We beached the canoe and unloaded. A log foot bridge to aid backpackers across the river was suspended above the rapids, and we lugged our gear in shifts, crossing and recrossing the bridge, hauling the gear up the knoll to camp.

We pitched our small tent and set up an elaborate system of waterproof tarps over it. We gathered firewood, being sure to minimally impact the forest, picking only dry wood, long dead. We didn't put an ax to anything. Instead, we broke larger branches by leveraging them between two trees or stepping on them. We gathered fine shavings of yellow birch bark for starter.

Chores complete, we sat on the foot bridge. The swiftly moving water created cool updrafts that dispersed the bugs. It was delightful to rest there, legs dangling, bathed in cool vapors with hardly a bug in sight. Things were definitely looking up. So it was with great contentment that I took a cup of water and sat down again on the bridge to brush my teeth as the sun went down and the air cooled. I don't have many teeth in my mouth. When I was a kid my parents were too poor to give me proper dental care, and in my early twenties, most of my teeth were pulled. Since that time, I've worn a full upper denture and a bottom partial.

On the bridge above the Oswegatchie that evening, somehow my toothbrush hooked on my bottom partial. It flipped from my hand, and I watched in disbelief as it sailed into the rapids, disappearing in the froth. How was I going to eat for the next six days? And the voice in my head said again, *Go home, fools, trouble waits!*

When I told Paulette about the partial she looked at me as if I might be cursed. That night, however, we slept like babes, and the next morning, bright and early, we hiked three miles into the old growth. The trail skirted marsh and wetlands, a fertile breeding ground for insects. We crossed the stream numerous times by skipping stones and walking on logs, our balance and steadiness tested.

Spectacular stands of white pine trees rewarded our perseverance. The canopy was high up in the sky. The forest was open in places with a deep carpet of pine needles. Sometimes our feet sank as much as four inches into the soft duff. In other areas, the woods were thick with a dense understory of young hemlocks. The place had an ancient silence, a depth, stillness, and magic that held me transfixed. It was a forest in its primeval state, untouched by man.

It would have been bliss to be there—but for the bugs. They enveloped us. Bug spray and our nets were only minimally effective against them. They were so bad that in desperation we hiked over a ridge to a pond that was marked on our map, thinking we'd jump in the water and escape. The hike down to the pond was heavy going through thick patches of hobblebush, and when we got there we couldn't face the thought of exposing our flesh. So we ended up crawling under a space blanket and lying there like besieged animals.

Such was our day. Still, I did get my photos, and I was much pleased when we got back to camp—a camp that was perfect but for one small, seemingly inconsequential detail.

As every woodsman knows, in bear country you're supposed to hoist your food at least ten feet off the ground. But we were canoe camping, stylin', and half our food was packed in a forty-eight-quart cooler, a cooler that, believe me, was not amenable to hoisting. The truth is, getting this cooler airborne had defied our ingenuity. After much to-do, I'd stashed it at the far end of camp, and tried to persuade Paulette that there weren't any bears around and, if there were, they'd leave us alone.

That night, snug in our tent, as I was about to doze off, Paulette grabbed me. "Something's in camp!" she whispered breathlessly into my ear.

Our flashlight was right by my head. I grabbed it, unzipped the mosquito netting at our feet, and shined it between the tent flaps. A big porcupine waddled off, the biggest Paulette and I had ever seen. A friend in the wild had come to visit us! I rezipped the net, put the flashlight back in its spot, got comfortable again and was drifting off, when Paulette shook me.

"Paul. Paul, I hear something!"

The porcupine was back. We watched it as it investigated everything in our camp, occasionally staring back at us, its black-tipped quills glistening. Finally, it lumbered off into the hemlock, and we curled in our sleeping bags, smiling at the thought of our benign night visitor.

I was falling asleep when Paulette shook me.

"Paul. There's something in camp!"

"It's only the porcupine."

"No it's not!" she said, teeth clenched.

Then I heard a big whooshing sound. I peered between the tent flaps. A pair of yellow eyes were looking at me—and those eyes were five feet off the ground!

"It's a bear!" I whispered. "There's a bear in our camp!"

I slipped from the tent and grabbed a canoe paddle. The bear was huffing, darting around the camp. I could feel its power and speed in the way its shoulders rolled, the quick, heavy push of its haunches. I waved the canoe paddle at it, beat the bushes, screamed and yelled. In a nearby tree, I thought that I heard claws clicking against bark. Cubs? I didn't have time to investigate. I jumped up and down and charged the bear. It bolted for the woods. Only then did I realize that I was naked. I clutched my paddle, trembling from the aftermath of the adrenaline that had flooded my body. No wonder that bear ran off—what a sight I was!

I ducked back into the tent. "I scared off the bear! But you know, it might have been a sow. I'm not sure, but I think I heard her cubs scrambling up a tree."

You might think that I was foolish to try to frighten a bear. Well, I wouldn't have done it if the bear had been a grizzly. Trying to intimidate a grizzly could have easily ended in my death. While you *can* intimidate a black bear, the type that inhabits the eastern United States, you don't want to run from it—this could trigger its predator tendencies, causing it to take chase. I had to do *something*, since letting the bear rummage through camp might have meant the destruction of our tent and gear.

I was now determined to get some sleep. It was a six-mile hike to the old growth area that we planned to explore the next day. But as I drifted off, Paulette shook me again. "Paul!" she said. "The bear is back!"

This time, I dressed and pulled on my boots. I was going to show that animal I meant business. I yelled and chased her, and she ran five feet up a tree and wouldn't budge. I screamed, growled, and brandished my paddle. She hugged the tree. She wouldn't leave. We were locked in a duet: she hovered on the cusp of fight or flee. So did I. Though I was doing more of the fighting, and the bear was doing more of the fleeing, still she defied me.

I took one of Paulette's sneakers and bounced it off the bear's broad back. This had an effect. She scuttled down the tree and disappeared into the night woods. But before I had time to catch my breath she was back, tearing through camp. She huffed, woofed, and mewed, strange sounds that raised the hair on the back of my neck. I whistled at her. My whistle is piercingly loud. She ran off but quickly returned. Each time I chased her away I had to get closer to her.

You know how you always wonder about your mate, your partner in life. Who is that person? Who is she really? What stuff is she made of? How is she going to react when you're in a dangerous situation? Will she be there by your side? Well, Paulette seemed incredible, calm as could be. Only one reaction gave away her fear.

"Paul," she said in an urgent whisper. "I have to go to the bathroom."

"You've got to be kidding!"

"No. I really have to go and I have to go *now.*"

Of course she wasn't going alone, so I had to come with her. And, of course, this being Paulette, who is scrupulous about not polluting the environment, we had to be at least two hundred feet away from the river before she would drop her drawers. That distance is hard to gauge in the dark, and Paulette likes to be on the safe side.

We traipsed into the woods. Paulette went to the bathroom. We traipsed back to camp. I confronted the bear *again,* and then there was another little tap on my shoulder.

"Paul, I need to go."

"But you just went!"

"I know but I need to go again, and I need to go *now*."

Other than that, Paulette was as cool as a cucumber.

"Let's let the bear have the camp for a little while," she suggested, at one point. "Maybe those really were cubs you heard, and she needs to get them back."

We crossed the river on the foot bridge and sat down in the darkness. How long should we wait, we wondered. We wanted to give the bear enough time to get her cubs down from the tree where I thought I had heard them. Were the cubs the problem? Were they why this bear was refusing to leave? We gave her a good long time to do whatever it was she needed to do, and it was well past midnight when we finally returned to inspect our camp. At first it looked like nothing was missing. *Great*, we thought. The bear has gotten her cubs and gone back into the woods, where she belongs. But then we noticed that the cooler was gone. Off in the distance, deep in the Adirondack night, we could hear bottles breaking and somebody enjoying herself.

We assessed the situation. We had only half our food left, and I had only half my teeth. We decided (or, more precisely, I decided) that we'd stick it out for a couple more days and get what photos we could. I was gratefully ensconced in my sleeping bag when Paulette shook me awake.

"Paul, the bear is back!" she hissed.

And sure enough, there was the bear, huffing and snorting and carrying on. We decided to light a fire.

In the primitive skills classes which I offer in my nature school, we teach fire making. In fact, we teach how to make bow drill fires— fires that you start by friction without using a match. I tell you this to establish my fire-making credentials and to illustrate how rattled I was. I could not start a fire that night to save my life. The wood just wouldn't go. The flames trickled for an instant and then faltered as the bear charged back and forth on the periphery of the fire circle. Finally, in desperation, I grabbed an emergency fire starter stick, shoved it under the wood, and put a match to it. These sticks are designed to start a fire in a hurricane, and the wood finally flared.

The bear did not bat an eye. It was not afraid of fire! Paulette and I looked at each other in disbelief. There was nothing left but to break camp and leave. And the voice inside me that had said, *Go home, fools, trouble waits,* was now saying, *I told you so.*

Quaking in my boots, half-crazed, exhausted, I kept the fire going and the bear at bay while Paulette broke camp and loaded the canoe.

Fog had rolled in, hanging over the river in a wet sheet that was so thick I couldn't see my hand in front of my face. Our head lanterns were useless—their light reflected by the mist only made visibility worse. With them on, we moved around like two gigantic yellow glowworms. The fog carried sound, and I lost my sense of distance. The river's hiss felt close, right next to my ear, and the bear's pawing and snorting and its heavy breath erupted unexpectedly, sometimes reassuringly far away and the next moment alarmingly close.

We were about to depart when Paulette said, "Wait! We can't leave with the fire going."

I thought she was insane. "Don't worry about the fire! It's got rocks around it, and besides, Smokey here will look after it."

"Nope," she said. "We can't leave until that fire is out."

In fairness, I must say that there was a drought that summer, which at least partially explained Paulette's insistence. I was caught between an intractable wife and an equally intractable bear. Guess who was elected to put the fire out.

I filled the canoe baler with river water. The bear was in the middle of the campsite, and it was clear that she now owned the place. I was defenseless, having nothing in my hands except a baler full of water. When the water hit the flames, it made a big whoosh! That scared the bear, and she tore back and forth, huffing and snorting.

"Nice bear," I said. "Nice bear." And that friendly voice inside me now said, *Don't run, Paul. Do not run.*

I retreated slowly, and Paulette and I pushed off in the canoe. The current carried us out from the bank and downstream, except it was hard to tell if we were traveling quickly or not at all. Canoeing in the dark is always a risky proposition, but that night it was doubly dangerous. Because of the fog, we were running blind. The river swirled against our gunnels, and we dipped into the head of one rapid and then another, riding the standing waves like a bobbing cork. We took a little water but otherwise emerged unscathed.

Then the river became still. We peered in the woods, trying to find a campsite. Suddenly, something was blasting through the woods toward the river. It was running directly at us! We heard a big splash. All we could think of was bear revenge! What was going on? Was this bear a remorseless force of nature? Our jaws dropped, and we sat through an ominous silence, drifting on the current in the dark, until suddenly, right next to us, there was an enormous splash—*kaboom!*

We both jumped. Our nerves were frayed! There were more splashes, and then we realized it was only beavers. They had run to the river when they heard us coming and now they were around our canoe, whopping the water with their tails. Every time they made a splash, we jumped out of our skins.

By the time we found another suitable campsite it was 3 A.M. We were shell-shocked, and mustered just enough energy to drag our canoe and gear up a steep bank, crawling on our hands and knees. Of course, Paulette insisted that we hoist our food, which we did like zombies. We pitched our tent, crawled into our sleeping bags, closed our eyes, and then—lightning! It flashed across the sky while thunder boomed overhead, shaking the ground. Paulette hates lightning. She was on her fingertips and toes in the tent. "If there's less of me on the ground, I'll be safer," she said.

This line of reasoning did not impress me. I barely had the energy to tell her to go to sleep. Finally, the storm abated and Paulette relaxed. We were about to fall asleep when it was me who jumped up screaming.

"The film!" I said. "The film was in the cooler! The bear took the cooler *and* my film." We now had to go back to our abandoned camp first thing in the morning, track the bear, and get the film. The photographs were all we had to show for what had turned into a hairraising fiasco.

The next morning dawned bright and hot. We'd had three hours of sleep.

We had an idea where the cooler might be from where we heard the bear feasting the night before. We soon found it, about two hundred yards back in the bush from our camp. Incisor bites marked the lid and sides. The bear was so dexterous that she had opened some of the bottles in the cooler without breaking them. She had very specific tastes. I can report that she clearly didn't like mustard or salsa. I retrieved my film, which was miraculously unscathed, despite bite marks through the Tupperware container that I kept it in. Finally (and by this time even I was more than ready), we headed out of the bush.

I wondered about that bear—how indomitable she seemed, her

persistence and odd behavior—until we went back into the same area the following summer with a group of tracking students. We spoke to a local who lived on the edge of the Five Ponds Wilderness.

"Oh, you must have got one of those dump bears," he said. It turned out that around the time of our bear incident a local dump had closed. A number of the Five Pond bears that had grown accustomed to feeding on garbage were suddenly left without a source of food. Those bears were desperate, and they were used to people. They were good at opening jars. They weren't afraid of fire. And suddenly that whole bizarre night made sense.

Fear has fascinated me all my life. As a child I was fearful. I had nightmares, and I was afraid of the dark. I'd lie in bed at night in my room. Cars passed on the country highway near our house. Headlights wavered through the trees, casting shadows on the wall, making me wonder what was lurking in the closet. God forbid my hand should stick out over the edge of the bed. Something might leap up and grab it! I made sure my legs were carefully tucked inside the blankets.

As I entered my early teens I wondered about fear. To a boy growing up in those days, it seemed that if you were macho, strong, and brave you were accepted and respected. If you weren't, you were scorned. You became an object of derision, or worse. I took many beatings from other kids because they sensed that I was afraid. I was labeled a sissy.

To compensate, I assumed a tough persona. I became the leader of youth gangs and then motorcycle gangs. I became the toughest streetfighter around. Although I wouldn't admit it to anybody, or to myself, for that matter, fear lurked under my macho persona. It stalked me. I felt I had to transcend fear, conquer it.

So I deliberately put myself in situations that challenged me. In my teens, before I discovered motorcycles, my passion was guns and hunting. It was all I talked about, all I thought about. I had a 16-gauge double-barrel sawed-off shotgun. When I fired that gun at close range, I couldn't miss. When I was about fifteen, I chose a night that was so dark that I couldn't see my hand in front of my face, and I took my gun, heading for the woods. I chose a trail that was so densely bordered with greenbriar and shrubbery that I couldn't stray off it. I started down that trail without a flashlight, inching along, sometimes stopping for long periods, adrenaline pumping. Do you know what it's like to have a grouse flush from under your feet, exploding like a bomb with all that adrenaline already in your system? I had to conquer fear. It made the difference between being accepted, belonging, having people look up to me, or being ostracized, isolated, and scorned. I could put on a good show, not only for others but also for myself. But way down, deep inside, I knew that I was still afraid.

In those days, it sometimes seemed to me that I structured my whole life to confront my fear, to try to conquer it. One of the main ways I did this was through fighting. In my early twenties, I was in a street fight that was a perfect example of the body reacting in a fight-or-flight response. The surge of adrenaline that helped me survive that fight was the same bodily response that helped me confront the bear years later in the Adirondacks.

I had traveled with my first wife and three friends on motorcycles from Westport, Massachusetts, to the Newport Jazz Festival. It was a night ride, set to the unmistakable soundtrack of three Harley-Davidsons with straight tailpipes. In those days, riding was the feeling closest to freedom: the wind in your hair, iron beneath you, a machine responding faithfully to each command, and a beautiful woman with her limbs wrapped around you, a constant reminder of her sensuousness.

The Harleys echoed for miles as we drove through the wooded valleys. Fresh countryside fragrances and abrupt temperature changes greeted us as we wove in and out of patches of ground fog that hugged the low spots. Riding didn't get much better than this.

Newport was packed. We parked our bikes and sauntered off through the fields toward the parking lots that ringed the festival. It was a public area, and people were milling about, going back and forth to their cars, standing in groups drinking beer, an early 1960s scene. But there was a feeling of danger in the air that night. Ron, one of my friends, had a long beard and wore leather pants, a leather jacket embossed with studs, and a motorcycle helmet with a skull painted on it. The mouth of the skull opened to reveal Ron's face. My other friend, Gillie, had bushy sideburns and long hair. He wore a hat like Marlon Brando's in *The Wild One*. I had one of those hats, too. Mine had all kinds of pins and studs in it. We all wore dark sunglasses, even at night. I had orange lenses that were good for night vision. My leather jacket was loaded with studs, and my kidney belt, a foot wide at the back, was decorated with over five hundred steel studs, which I had hammered into it myself. We wore engineer boots and tight jeans. We were in heavy biker mode—an outrageous-looking, attention-getting threesome. And attract attention we did.

Walking toward the concert area I realized that I had become separated from my two friends. I looked around. They were about forty feet away, being attacked by a gang of twenty guys in their teens. Ron was big, into lifting weights, and Gillie was a mean street fighter, tough and fast, but they still couldn't handle twenty teens.

When I saw my friends attacked, I didn't think. The adrenaline rushed through me, and my response was *fight*. I tore off and stormed into the gang, punching as hard and fast and as furiously as I could. Ron somehow escaped, and I saw Gillie tossed from man to man—hit, pushed, slapped. I thrashed out, trying to do as much damage as I could, break some jaws and noses with my fists. In my fury, I attracted attention, and now the gang turned on me.

Everything was happening fast. Fists hit me in rapid fire. The gang tossed me all over the place. I found myself slipping toward the ground, bashing my attackers with fists, elbows, and knees, struggling to keep myself upright even as they pummeled me toward the black pavement of the parking lot. I felt my feet go out from under me, and I heard the teenagers roaring with rage and triumph, the kind of cry that people think of as "wild" but I do not see as wild at all. Adrenaline sang full force inside me, rendering painless the blows, somehow giving me strength. I hauled myself under the bottom of a metal fence on the lot's edge so that only the lower half of my body was a target. Soon the kids grew bored and left.

Earlier, I had felt something break in my shoulder. I had felt and heard a sickening snap inside my body but hadn't actually felt pain. I had known that what was happening was bad, but adrenaline had shielded me. The arm hung useless. I couldn't move it. My friends had abandoned me. My wife appeared, helping me to my feet, my mouth bloody, a shooting pain in my head.

This was the same adrenaline that I'd felt pulsing through me when I confronted the bear. It may have saved my life by enabling me, in what now seems like a superhuman effort, to pull myself under that fence. What other people see as a fear response—the release of adrenaline—I believe is actually the body's intelligent response to danger.

Through being what was considered brave and daring—fighting—I was viewed by my peers as fearless. But no matter how many fights I was in, I eventually came to realize that this macho role my friends and I were playing was superficial. We were so boisterous, so tough, because we were afraid not to be. It was a monstrous charade that everybody bought. The underlying motivation, the whole basis of our life in the gang, was fear. Fear led us to put on this mask of machismo.

The fear we felt in the gang was not the fear of the animal in the forest responding to danger. It was not the fear, let's call it *body* fear, that I felt the night I wrestled the bear. Wrestling the bear was the intelligent bodily response to danger. But there's a very different sort of beast that disguises itself as that appropriate bodily response. This other beast I'll call *psychological* fear. Psychological rather than body fear is a reactive mechanism that separates us from our essential nature. Psychological fear does not exist in the moment. It only exists in the future. If you're absolutely present, living the moment, there is no psychological fear.

To illustrate this point, imagine someone is pointing a gun at you. You're not afraid because a gun is pointed at you, you're afraid because you might get shot. If you're being shot, you're not afraid that you're being shot, you're afraid that you'll be shot again. If you're shot again, you're not afraid that you're being shot again, you're afraid you might die.

We're talking about fear that is a product of thought. As humans, we have an incredible facility of intellect, of the thought process, which we tend to think of as an asset. But thought can also be a curse.

Unknowingly and sometimes uncontrollably, we create fear. We create situations that project danger (for example, when we think we may look foolish or suffer humiliation), spurring the body to produce adrenaline, often when that fight-or-flight response is not appropriate.

What is this fear's root? How do we move beyond it? How do we save it for those moments when we wrestle the bear, when it is appropriate, instead of living with it day in and day out? Our vitality is undermined by nagging fears about our futures, our position in the world. These fears eat away at us. They create inner conflict and activate our adrenals inappropriately until we come to feel the state that I see in so many people these days—an underlying malaise, a sense of exhaustion. When people come to my workshops to connect with nature, some are striving, whether they know it or not, to put fear back in its place.

Hang out with your fear when you're feeling afraid. Follow its movement. Become intimate with it. Fear is an opportunity. Approach it like a tracker in the forest—watch where it goes, what it does, what it eats, where it rests, where it turns, where it stops, where it hides. Embrace it. Stay with it.

You may find, as you track fear through your inner wilderness, that it's a little island. In order for fear to exist it has to separate itself. Its existence is dependent on division, on isolation. It has separated itself from the thought process. It disguises itself as the thinker of the thought, when in reality it is just a thought.

Let's go back to that self of my motorcycle days—the self that thought of itself as the leader of the pack, the self that thought it was brave, that had worked so hard to project a macho image. The satisfaction and the power that circled around that sense of self were immense. That self substantiated itself, at least in part, by communicating itself to others. And in that substantiation and communication there was a great sense of accomplishment.

When people accepted that macho self, I had a sense of well-being and power. The sense of well-being was dependent on that acceptance. If something threatened that projection of self, my invincible machismo, if I made one mistake, if I appeared for even an instant slightly weak, then all the power and all the pleasure and my whole sense of well-being were threatened. There was fear. My so-called bravery was built on an image, and it was therefore dependent on that image for its survival. That image had to be maintained and defended rigorously. The energy holding up my machismo was the movement of fear.

If our well-being depends on who we *think* we are, then our well-being will of necessity be threatened because our self is a thought, a construct, an idea, a projection. The underlying movement of life is always undermining its foundation, like waves lapping against pilings, pulling away at the sand in which they're anchored.

To understand this, let's look at the most graphic example of psychological fear and how it is confused with body fear—our fear of death. Think of the moment of your death. What do you feel? Now ask yourself, what is this self that you have so elaborately constructed and fought so hard to enhance and maintain? What is this self you are so fearful of losing, that you spend so much of your life energy struggling to maintain? Who is it that's afraid to die?

Glimmering on the edge of death, sweeping in to overwhelm us, is the larger sense of who we are. It is there all the time inside us, but we avoid it with our fear, with the image of who we think we are. This larger self is what I call the wild within, the whole of the conscious universe. In that expansive awareness of our larger identity there is no fear, and if we watch fear from that place—not trying to conquer or control it but just understand it—then fear will start to atrophy. It will diminish and shrivel, perhaps not immediately but inevitably.

The Kogi Indians of Colombia had a method for bringing the future leaders of their society to a larger, more embracing sense of self. They selected from the community very young boys, less than one year old, and put them in a cave. There was just enough light in the cave so that the boys' eyesight would not be destroyed as they grew. But for years these select children never saw the outside world. They never saw the world of nature.

The old men, the enlightened ones at the end of their lives, would explain to the children in great detail what the world looked like. Then, at age nine, the boys would be brought outside, and all the things that they had ever been told about the outside world would fall at their feet as a leaf among billions. Their senses smelled, saw, heard, and tasted the real world—the fragrance of a flower, the song of a bird, the dance of a butterfly in the sunlight—and suddenly, nothing that had been told to these children had meaning. This put their intellect in its place, in its corner. These young boys were living the wild within.

The following exercise, which I call Stone Meditation, will help you see how psychological fear operates. Have you ever stepped from stone to stone to get across a river or stream? Have you ever watched someone do this? Some people make it look easy. They don't hesitate. They seem to glide across the water, from stone to stone. Other people are full of hesitation. They look awkward. They test each stone before putting their full weight on it. They usually end up falling into the water. The difference between those two types is one type has psychological fear, the other doesn't.

In order to do this exercise, set aside twenty minutes. Find a stream with stones that are close enough together to walk or jump across. Look at the path across the water. The possibility of falling and getting cold and wet will enhance the fear factor. If there's no stream nearby, set some sturdy wooden boxes in a row and look at the row as a path you want to cross. Now, skip across the stones or boxes. Don't skip on wet or slippery stones.

The process of skipping from stone to stone or box to box will demand your full attention. You should be solidly aware of each stone. Move slowly at first. There is no hurry. You're not going anywhere. This exercise will bring you out of your head, out of your intellect, where psychological fear is, and down into your body.

Start with a fifteen-minute routine. You can eventually build up to an hour. This exercise teaches bodily awareness, confidence, and agility. It is also a good exercise for learning about being present and aware. You will be presented with opportunities to see just what brings you away from the moment and out of your body. The distracting factor will most likely be the movement of thought, when it expresses itself as fear or just starts to move. It will pull you away from your stones, and you may lose your balance. Be careful.

Thought may also try to take the helm. It will try to tell the body where to go or how to do it. You will likely find that thought is a hindrance and that when it is quiet, a greater intelligence takes over.

When thought drops away, when there is just the body moving with this greater intelligence, you will be flying. Your feet will move by themselves. You'll be free from the inhibitions of thought, free from psychological fear—the bear that we wrestle inside us that causes us so much pain and grief.

3.

LOONS AND THE
LESSONS OF LOVE

So long as you are compelled to do something because

it is your duty you don't love what you are doing.

When there is love there is no duty . . .

—J. KRISHNAMURTI,

FREEDOM FROM THE KNOWN

STILL WATER, EARLY MORNING ON QUABBIN RESERVOIR, 1987. I listen to loons tremolo and wail. The sound of their calls transports me into a state of primordial calm. Their calls fade gradually away, echoing off the surrounding hills. I am overcome by the stillness and silence that follow. It seems palpable, tingling, as if each molecule of air is suddenly shimmering on its edge. It is a silence that communicates directly to me of the wonder of being alive and the gift of life. The loons by their calls are able to summon from deep inside me an intense love for the wilderness.

I had taken a job as a loon warden on Quabbin in the spring of 1984. At this time, loons were a species of special concern in Massachusetts, a state in the southernmost part of the loons' breeding range. There were only a handful of loons nesting in the whole state, and there was an effort by the government to make sure those loons succeeded in breeding and producing chicks.

Quabbin had several nest sites to which mated pairs of loons returned each spring after wintering in coastal areas. I had volunteered to watch over those loons, but as often happens when you volunteer for projects, sooner or later you're likely to find yourself hired for a paying job. If you're a good enough volunteer, before you know it, the powers that be realize you're indispensable.

In 1984, loons were in decline over much of the North American continent. They faced many hazards: coexistence on lakes with boats, ingestion of lead sinkers, contamination of fresh water in their breeding grounds, loss of their habitat to development, loss of fish prey to acid precipitation, and fluctuating water levels on lakes managed for electric power or for drinking water.

There are five different loon species: the Pacific, Arctic, red-throated, yellow-billed, and common loon, which is the kind I observed in Quabbin. All loons love to eat fish. Minnows, sticklebacks, and small perch are some of their favorites. Loons have nests on fresh-water lakes during the spring/summer breeding season. Most of the available literature says that they lay one to two eggs each season. I've seen them with three. Chicks hatch twenty-eight to thirty days after the eggs are laid.

Common loon chicks are able to fly when they're about twelve weeks old. Then both adults and juveniles leave the lakes together to winter at sea off the coasts of California, western Florida, and the Atlantic seaboard. Common loons breed across much of North America: on the edges of the tundra, the upper Great Lakes region, and in New England. Small numbers breed in the Rocky Mountains, as far south as Yellowstone National Park. They also nest in Iceland, the British Isles, Scandinavia, and continental Europe, and they winter off the Atlantic and Mediterranean coasts of the European continent.

Loons have a certain power and mystique, to which I am not immune. They're one of the most ancient birds in the world. So old, in fact, that they still have solid bones. Their bones are heavy, compared to the featherweight hollow bones of most birds. They have small wings compared to their bodies, relative to other birds. Combine their weight and wing design, and you can imagine the size of the open water area that loons need for takeoff, sometimes as much as a quarter mile. It looks like loons run on the water before they become airborne. But once they lift off, they fly very fast. They've been clocked at speeds of up to ninety miles per hour.

These birds look ancient. In their breeding plumage, common loons have black heads with bright red eyes. When the sun hits those eyes right, they look like rubies lit from behind. There's an eeriness as well as a beauty to them. Under their chins loons have two white bands of feathers that wrap like jewelry around their necks. Most of their plumes are iridescent jet black. The back feathers that cover their wings have white checkerboards on them. Their sides are dotted with dark gray and white spots.

Common loons have four different vocalizations: wails, yodels, tremolos, and hoots. A loon usually wails in order to contact another loon. Only males yodel; each male's yodel has a distinct signature of pitch and phrasing. When males claim their territories each spring, they announce themselves with this yodel. The tremolos, the sounds usually associated with loons, often occur when the birds are agitated or disturbed. Finally, there are hoots. These are soft little sounds, intimate calls that usually occur between a mated pair or between a parent and chick.

I felt guilty that I was getting paid to be a loon warden because I loved the job so much. My days involved leisurely cruises in a state-provided sixteen-foot boat to determine how many loons were nesting on the lake and where they were. Most of the nests were on small islands. My job was to watch the nests from shore with a powerful spotting scope and find out when the loons laid their eggs. I needed to know when those eggs were going to hatch because I had to make sure the nests were not disturbed while the eggs were hatching and when the chicks were newborn.

Loons are secretive creatures, and they are almost always intolerant of intrusions into their private domain. So as not to disturb them, I had to observe their nests from a distance, and watch their comings and goings, breeding, hatching of eggs, and rearing of young. If they were disturbed, there was the possibility that they would abandon their nests.

The job started in early spring, since loons would come to Quabbin as soon as the reservoir was free of ice. The males came first to claim their territory by yodeling and chasing other loons from their domain. Their territories were sometimes as large as a quarter of a square mile. The loons always selected the same nest site or nesting area that they had used in prior years. That helped me find their nests. Quabbin's water level fluctuates, and sometimes the loons would come to an island on which they had nested the previous year that was now under water. So I'd search the surrounding islands to see where they were going to pop up.

Hanging out with the loons over the course of three seasons, it was amazing how intimate I became with them. I came to see that each had a personality. Some would be very nervous about any encroachment into their territory, especially from a motorboat. Others appeared quite serene. Because their legs are situated far back on their torso, loons can't walk. In fact, on land they push and pull themselves along with their feet and wings, bellies rubbing against the ground. Their awkwardness on land makes them vulnerable and skittish, to differing degrees. A boat might be one thousand feet away and a particular pair of loons will bolt from their nest into the water. Another pair might tolerate a boat coming to an outrageous fifteen feet from their nest before they bolt.

A bolting loon is a hazard to its eggs—it can inadvertently drag them into the water. If that happens, the pair will not be able to get the eggs back into the nest. A bolting loon may also crush its eggs, which I saw happen more than once.

Part of my job was to protect the loons. People can easily end up loving loons to death. It's not that they want to hurt loons, but sometimes they don't know to keep far enough away. If someone comes too close to a nest, loons will see that as a threat. They may start to do a penguin dance, which looks like the loon is running on the water, flapping its wings, and tremoloing. This is an extremely photogenic fuss, and I've seen people come closer and closer to a loon's nest, shooting pictures, not understanding that the loon is telling them in no uncertain terms to please vacate its territory.

Sometimes my morning would start off with an incredibly flat mirrorlike lake—so flat, so pristine, so virgin, so still that it felt like it would be a sacrilege to move through it. The silence was so intense that I hated to start up the motor. I was always in a hurry to stop the boat, stop the motor, stop the noise; to just be there in that incredible stillness, listening for a wail of a loon or the soft little hoots of geese in the distance. The silence and the mirror-like water seemed to say, "Stop. Do not enter. Sacred space."

Sometimes there would be morning fog on the still water that would slowly burn away with the rising sun. The fog swirling in the air, transforming the early morning light into luminous curtains and strange shapes, made me think that a sorcerer had cast a spell over the water and that I was entering other realms, other worlds. But, of course, it wasn't other worlds, just our planet Earth. The sounds of the loons in the fog carried for miles. Even a loon half a mile away sounded like it was right next to my boat.

A pair of loons had nested in the Hop Brook area of Quabbin on a piece of land that changed with the reservoir's water level. In spring, when the water was high, it was a small island, and the loons nested on its outer part, out in the lake, close to a channel that separated their island from another island about fifty feet away.

When the water level dropped, the island became a peninsula. Raccoons could get out there, and two years in a row the coons had raided the loons' nest and eaten the eggs. There was also another danger to this nest. Between the two islands was a channel right next to the nest. The channel led to a small secluded cove, an excellent spot for fishing. Fishermen would drive their motorboats right through that little channel between the two islands, scaring the loons off the nest. The loons couldn't see the fishermen coming until the last minute, and then they would bolt off the nest.

During the spring and early summer of my third year on the job, I studied that nest long and hard. I felt particularly protective of these loons, and one day, I saw that there were eggs in the nest. I had a sense of foreboding, counting out the twenty-eight to thirty days of gestation. Sure enough, the eggs were due to hatch over the July Fourth weekend, Quabbin's busiest time.

I made sure that I was watching the nest on that weekend. It was an anxious, exciting time. For three consecutive years, I'd watched these loons establish their territory and build their nest. I'd watched them take turns sitting on their eggs, mouths agape, breathing hard to keep themselves cool in the hot sun. For two years they had failed to have chicks, and now the magic hour approached. Then I saw it: the smallest little thing emerged, about the size of a newly hatched baby chicken, all fuzzy and black. At first, all I saw was its tiny black head.

Only one loon was tending the nest when the chick hatched. I didn't know where the other loon was, and I didn't know whether it was the male or female on the nest. About three hours after the chick hatched, I saw a motorboat approaching the channel between the islands. I was horrified. I didn't want the loon to bolt off its nest and damage the newborn chick.

I jumped up and down on shore, waving at the boat. I don't know if they saw me. I ran out to the peninsula to try to warn the boat off. I was too late. The boat went through the channel quite fast. I motioned to the boat to approach me and explained the situation to the fishermen, who quickly motored away. I ran as fast as I could back to my spotting scope, breathless by the time I arrived.

I couldn't see the chick. The loon was in the water. It started to move slowly back to the nest. It acted strangely as it approached the nest. It kept putting its beak close to the area on the side of the nest where I had last seen the chick. It started to tremolo and wail, wail and tremolo. Finally, from across the water, I heard an answering wail. The other bird flew in.

One loon sat on the nest while the other swam back and forth in the cove. Both birds were agitated, tremoloing in unison. The bird on the nest put its beak close to where I had last seen the chick. It got on and off the nest several times. Both loons swam back and forth, tremoloing. The sound broke my heart. They actually took off together, which is rare, tremoloing, only to come back and take off again.

One of the last times that they took off, I ran to the nest. I had a strong suspicion of what I would find. There was the chick, limp and crushed. It had been run over when its parent bolted off the nest when the boat had come through the channel.

The bond that these loons shared and all their hard work resulted only in a third year of tragedy. Looking down at the dead chick, hearing the loons tremolo in duet, was a powerful, affecting moment. I looked at the loons and saw their commitment to each other, to their dead chick, to the eggs that had been eaten by raccoons, to the continuance of their own species, and to their progeny.

This is what some people think of as love: sex, bonding, commitment to family, regeneration of the species. In our mythology of the origin of love we might see the loons and their dogged persistence on their embattled nest as the crucible from which love emerges. In other words, the ancient loons are exhibiting in the animal or proto-human world the traits that we as human beings have embellished and called love. Like our loons, we tend to think that if two people are really in love, then they will be committed to each other, committed to their relationship, and that the relationship will last unto death.

Scientists might say that the loons' behavior has nothing to do with love as we know it. The loons' monogamy, their "committed" relationship, has to do with perpetuating their species and the distress they "feel" or, to be more precise, that they seem to exhibit at the death of their chick, is biological programming.

I don't want to argue this point, except to say that most of the ways in which we think about love, or even experience love, have been programmed, too. Sometimes what passes for love between two people is not really love at all. Most people enter into what I would call ideological love: in other words, some idea of love. They have this idea that they love each other, and they promise to be committed, to love each other and take care of each other forever. They make a verbal, ideological commitment, setting up an authority that dictates their behavior. That's what an ideology is—an authority. The ideology of marriage dictates commitment, fidelity, steadfastness, and loyalty. These are not bad traits in and of themselves, but sometimes they don't come from the heart. They're not real. People sometimes feel compelled to struggle and twist themselves into contortions because they feel this is what they're supposed to do, that this is how they're supposed to live . . . and love. To use Krishnamurti's language, people often end up in conflict between the "what should be" and the "what is." No wonder our closest relationships can sometimes cause us the most grief and pain.

Too often, images that people have of themselves and of each other are having what they think of as a relationship founded on an idea they call love. But it is our images, ideologies, and misperceptions that prevent us from understanding the true meaning of love.

Love is not an idea or an ideological commitment. It's not about images, and it is, most emphatically, not about self. It is not about the self experiencing something. It is not a feeling. Love is not the feeling, *I am in love.* It may be painful to say and painful to recognize, but love is not that delirious emotion that so many of us spend so much time and energy pursuing. Love is understanding what love is not.

Think of how a parent protects a child. Think of the toil of the loons and their incredible investment in their nest. Think of our love toward our children or the love your parents had for you. Think of the sometimes very possessive nature of that love, how it can want to manipulate a child to fit a parent's vision of that child becoming a doctor, a lawyer, or following some other prestigious career. How much does our child's success or nonsuccess affect how we feel about ourselves? Are we loving the child itself or the image of what we want our child to be? When we get what love is *not* out of the way, then genuine caring, genuine concern has room to breathe and space to exist.

In a sense, this pair of loons was able to let go of their tragedy three years in a row, and start over again. How many of us would have been able to rebound from such an experience? It is perhaps the hardest thing to let go of the death of a child, to move past that grief. Fortunately, I have never had to experience that; but I have had to work through another kind of painful and difficult letting go that had to do with love. This experience brought me closer to the true nature of love, teaching me that love is about letting go of images.

Back in the late 1970s, I had come to a place in my life where I really wanted to understand love. I had gone through several years of spiritual inquiry, studied various religions, and founded and lived in an ashram. I had an intense interest in discovering who I was, about understanding and delving deeply into the interconnectedness of all things. A part of this was wanting to understand—not intellectually but deeply, down to every last cell in my body—the meaning of love.

I asked life, Please give me the lessons I need to learn deeply the meaning of love. I don't care how much I have to suffer. I accept whatever it is I have to go through.

It seemed like a very simple request. Maybe my idea of myself and certain values that I thought I cherished would have to die in order for me to learn the meaning of love. I don't know if my questions had anything to do with what happened shortly afterward, but, in retrospect, maybe they did. I asked life to show me the true meaning of love, and life answered me. What an answer!

I was living with a woman I'll call Donna; we had a two-year-old daughter. I loved Donna deeply, and when our child came along I was really ready to be a father, fully and completely a father. But Donna fell in love with another man. When I found out about this, although I hadn't felt anger for many years, anger did arise. I felt it like never, ever before. It *was* my whole being. It was who I was. The anger was disgusting and debilitating. It was dark and blind. There was no way I could live with that anger. I had no choice. All I could do was to love Donna and to let go.

I left my home and most of my belongings to Donna and my child. I was devastated! Not only had I lost my partner, I'd lost a daughter—the person I had come closer to than almost any person in my life. Having to leave her was one of the most difficult things I've ever done. There was a lot of letting go to do.

I had an agreement with Donna that I could see my daughter at any time. But it's not the same when you can't tuck her in every night, see her in the morning, when your relationship is relegated to weekends and you're always saying good-bye. I had to walk away from an awful lot. It's one thing to talk about detachment. It's another thing to experience it.

I don't know if my talk with life had anything to do with putting me in this situation, but here I was. This was the second time around for me, since I'd already lost one family when my first wife Rosemary and I divorced and she moved away with our two children. With Donna, I had once again lost everything that meant anything to me. Sometimes, before going to sleep in my Volkswagen camper at night, I would cry out for the woman that I loved and for our child. I felt an actual tearing, as if my flesh itself were tearing.

The pain was deep and strong. But I was not angry with the pain. The pain wasn't something that I was fighting. I wasn't angry about my situation or disgusted with my life. My loss was an opportunity to learn about detaching, about giving something up. I embraced it. I did not push it away, I did not suppress it. I just cried. Fully, completely, loudly. I let the pain move through me, until it moved into every cell, until it penetrated every aspect of who I was.

When we live our lives pursuing pleasure and avoiding pain, we only live half our lives. When we try to avoid the other half, the suppression of pain makes us insensitive, dull, rigid. In my situation with Donna I could have looked at my life and said, This is bad. This is really bad. This shouldn't be happening. My life is destroyed. I watch people doing this all the time. Something goes wrong: a relationship ends, they suffer a setback, and they think their life is destroyed.

There's a story to illustrate the deceptive quality of this kind of thinking. The tale demonstrates that it's hard to know whether the events in one's life are bad or good.

Once upon a time there was a very old Chinese farmer. He lived on a farm, and had a horse and a son. Without them he would never have been able to manage the farm. Respected by people from miles around, he was known as a wise man, and when people needed help or advice, they would seek him out.

One day the old man's horse ran away and didn't return. The man and his son searched high and low, hither and yon for the horse, but they couldn't find it. It had seemingly vanished into thin air. When the neighbors found out about the horse's disappearance, they came to see the old man and console him.

"Old man," they said, "we're really sorry to hear about your

horse running away. What are you going to do? You need the horse to work your farm. What bad luck!"

The old man looked at them and said, "Good luck, bad luck. Who knows?"

The neighbors didn't know what to make of that answer, but the old man refused to say more and they left. A couple of days later they heard that the old man's horse had come back and brought a wild horse with it. Now the old man had two horses.

Well, the neighbors were so happy for the old man, they were back at his place the next day telling him, "Old man, we're so glad to hear about your good luck. Now you have two horses."

The old man looked at them and said, "Good luck, bad luck. Who knows?"

The neighbors didn't know what to make of the old man. They had a lot of respect for him, but they didn't understand why he wasn't happy and excited with this unexpected stroke of good fortune.

The next day they heard that the old man's son was trying to break in the wild horse when he fell from the horse and broke his leg. The neighbors converged on the old man. They were adamant.

"Old man," they said, "surely now you must admit this is bad luck. This is your son we're talking about. How are you going to take care of him and take care of your farm? You were dependent on him. Certainly this is terribly bad luck."

But the old man just looked at them with a slight smile on his face. "Good luck, bad luck. Who knows?"

The neighbors were frustrated. They didn't understand the old man. They went back to their homes, only to find that the next day the army came through the area taking all able-bodied young men to go fight in a terrible war. The parents of these young men were *devastated. They knew many of their sons would not return. Of course, the army couldn't take the old man's son because he had a broken leg. The neighbors were overjoyed. They rushed back to the old man's house.*

"Old man," they said, "surely you must admit that this *is good luck."*

But the old man looked at them and said, "Won't you ever learn? Good luck, bad luck. Who knows?"

The story of the Chinese farmer expresses an understanding that bad and good are a continuum. A situation that seems to be catastrophic can actually be a profound opportunity to learn important life lessons. In the case of Donna and my experience with the loons, I learned lessons about love, loss, and letting go.

A few years after my breakup with Donna, Paulette came into my life. When people experience the kind of hurt and pain we have been talking about, they sometimes suppress and reject that pain and find it very hard to love again. But if I want to fully and completely experience the joys of Paulette, if I want to embrace her fully, I can't just embrace half of her. If I want to experience all of life fully and completely, I can't embrace half of life. In order to love, I have to embrace the joy and the pain all at the same time. Otherwise, I'm holding back something, afraid I might be hurt, not letting myself go completely because I'm afraid that she might be taken away.

Paulette may die. There may be another man. I may die. And in any of those events there would be great pain, which I don't want to experience again. But without taking the risk I can't love again either. I've learned that the only way to love is to love completely and with total abandonment.

We can start to see that the avoidance of discomfort can be a real hindrance to being able to fully embrace our lives. What can we do about this? Simply, learn to live with discomfort.

When I taught hatha yoga, I and a few other teachers had a slightly different philosophical twist. We concentrated on becoming flexible, not only physically but also psychologically. A posture that illustrates what I'm talking about is a variation of a standing forward bend. You can try this yourself. Stand with your feet parallel to each other and about shoulder-width apart. Clasp your hands behind your back, just at or above your buttocks. Keep your arms straight. Be aware of your breath and continue to breathe throughout the exercise. Bend your knees very slightly so that they aren't locked. Now slowly bend forward from the waist, keeping your back straight. As you move forward, bring your clasped hands out and away from your back and over your head as far as possible. Breathe in a slow, steady, even rhythm.

The objective is to go as far forward into the posture as you can to the point where you start to experience some discomfort, but not pain. It's important not to push this exercise too far. You don't want to injure yourself. There is a delicate balance here. Stay with the discomfort for a minute or two. You might notice that your breath is more labored, but just keep breathing. Don't hold it in. Slowly come out of the posture and relax, letting your breath return to normal.

And there you are. After a few minutes, you're completely comfortable again. Your whole body has smoothed out. But to gain flexibility, both physically and psychologically, you need to learn to leave that comfort. Back into the posture. Back into the discomfort. Learn to live with it. Learn to accept it. Embrace it. Relax with it.

In this movement back and forth between comfort and discomfort, the whole play of life is made clear and accentuated. Discomfort is just discomfort, whether it's psychological or physical. Whether you're jogging, holding a yoga posture, or lifting weights, try to find some kind of exercise to challenge you and put you into a place of discomfort. Whatever exercise you choose, be conscious that it is good medicine. Don't tune out. Don't put on earphones. Be with it. This doesn't mean becoming masochistic, it's just part of embracing and living life to the fullest extent.

Love is not *feeling*. It is not what we normally associate with "being in love": the excitement, euphoria, and desire that we tend to think of as the most desirable state of being possible, when we are at our happiest and most alive. Desire is not love. Yearning is not love. Love knows no attachment, no desire. It does not hope or grasp or strive. It is not about action or will. It cannot be about striving for unity or wholeness. As Krishnamurti explains in *Commentaries on Living*:

> *Love is not sensation; it is a flame without smoke. You will know love when you as the thinker are not. You cannot sacrifice yourself, the thinker, for love. There can be no deliberate action for love, because love is not of the mind. The discipline, the will to love, is the thought of love; and the thought of love is sensation. Thought cannot think about love, for love is beyond the reaches of the mind. Thought is continuous, and love is inexhaustible. That which is inexhaustible is ever new, and that which has continuance is ever in the fear of ending. That which ends knows the eternal beginning of love.*

Love is not a matter of choice, loving this but not that, loving what gives us pleasure and hating what gives us pain. Love is not a state of conflict, where we are trying to bend life to meet our desires. Desire is wanting things to be a certain way. That means a life of conflict, and love is not a life of conflict.

If I have a deep understanding of love, the kind that Krishnamurti talks about, which is inexhaustible and forever new, then when I learn to love one person, I have embraced everyone. It is love that is not about a particular relationship but is about the nature of all relationships, the relationship we have with life where there is no bias, where there is an unconditional acceptance of what life offers us. This acceptance embraces both pain and joy. Love is wisdom and freedom from the constraints of desire. It is about a falling away of self.

Love is not something "you" attain to. Love blows "you" away like a candle in a cyclone. But in the same breath, in the place of who you thought you were, it leaves the gifts of freedom, wisdom, and the fullness of life.

4.

STALKING

SILENCE

STALKING SKILLS ARE A CRUCIAL PART OF A HUNTER'S repertoire. Stalking involves inching your way through the forest, spending more time stopped than moving, all the while being incredibly attentive to and aware of everything around you.

I have adapted this age-old hunting skill in a special class on stalking that I teach in my tracking programs. In my teaching, stalking is not a means to get close enough to animals to be able to shoot them, but rather to see wildlife before it sees you. This can lead to dramatic encounters.

Beyond this, I teach stalking as meditation. At its core, stalking has more to do with stillness than with movement. It is about slowing down and blending in. It is the ability to melt into the forest.

Stalking allows people to drop their everyday personae, until the forest no longer realizes that they're there. When you *become* the forest, when you're silent inwardly and outwardly, the forest starts to wake up, to move. It's amazing what can happen.

In order to melt into the forest, a quality of attention is necessary to allow what you normally think of as "you" to disappear, like the Cheshire Cat in Lewis Carroll's *Alice in Wonderland*. When what's "you" disappears, something else, something that is larger and intensely alive, comes to the fore. This is the wild within.

In a typical stalking program, my students will meet me around noon in a parking area in front of a gate to the Quabbin Reservation, a large tract of wild land surrounding a reservoir that is a thirty-minute drive from my home in northcentral Massachusetts. I like to open this program with a powerful example that illustrates the importance of camouflage—an exercise that's much more effective than anything I could say to express my point.

I'd get to the parking area early, before anyone else, park my Jeep, and leave a big sign on its windshield that said: YOUR PROGRAM HAS BEGUN. YOU MUST FIND YOUR INSTRUCTOR. HE IS WATCHING YOU. I'd don full camouflage, including a face mask, a net that completely enveloped my head, with two narrow slits for my eyes. Then I'd hide myself in the woods, carefully picking my spot.

The woods around Quabbin are a mix of hardwoods and conifers. I'd find a thick patch of witch hazel, briar, and dense hemlock saplings close to the parking area. When I say close, I mean close—no more than ten feet from the lot. I made sure there were lots of branches to break my silhouette and something behind me, rocks, trees, or shrubbery, to hide my form. I'd push myself into a dense thicket, sweep the leaves aside, and put a pad on the ground to sit on.

One particular program took place in late October. The leaves were already mostly off the trees. The earth was chilly and wet. I was going to have to sit here for a long time, and I wanted to be comfortable. I piled the leaves that I'd swept aside on top of me and threw branches on top of myself as well. Then I waited.

The first student arrived. He had been on one of my previous programs, and recognized my Jeep. He read the sign that I'd put on the windshield. Immediately, he started looking around. Soon after, another car pulled into the parking area.

"Hey, read the sign, we've got to find him!" I heard the first student say. They both started walking the perimeter of the parking area, peering into the woods, at times almost stepping on me. One by one the other students arrived and joined the search (my stalking classes are limited to six; when you're stalking animals you can't have a big crowd).

I watched them as they foundered around, trying to find me. They looked right past me. They didn't even check the clump of trees that I was hidden in. It was as if their brains were telling them, "There's no way he's there."

They started poking around in the woods. They looked up in the trees. There was a culvert nearby. I heard one of them say, "No sense in going over there. He says he's watching us so he can't be inside that culvert!"

This game of hide and seek continued. My students dispersed in the woods. Nobody was left in the parking lot. I couldn't see the group anymore, but I could hear them thrashing about, the sounds growing softer and softer as they moved away from the parking lot and from my hiding place.

"Turkeys!" I yelled to them.

"I heard him! He called us turkeys!"

When you hear just one word, it's usually very difficult to figure out where it's coming from. They still had no idea where I was.

"Turkeys!" I yelled again.

This time they clued in. "It sounds like he's back toward the cars!" someone said.

They moved back in my direction, but still couldn't find me. They were not looking in the right places because their brains had told them there was no way I could be where I was. It's an interesting phenomenon: how we think can actually disrupt or impair our seeing what's around us.

The students were close to me, but they still weren't zeroing in. "Cluck, cluck, cluck!" I said. "Gobble, gobble!"

"He's right near here," one student said.

"I can't believe it!" said another.

"Gobble, gobble!"

They zeroed in on the noise, but I was still invisible to them. If I hadn't kept gobbling, I don't know how long it would have taken them to find me. Suddenly, one of them saw me.

"There he is!"

There was an uproar of disbelief.

"I can't believe it!" I heard from all sides.

I emerged from my spot, shedding leaves and branches. Now my students were psyched. They had come to do an animal stalking program, which, as they knew from the registration materials that I had sent them, is all about seeing and awareness. They had just had the experience of looking past something—a profound lesson in not seeing, in being unaware.

We gathered by the Quabbin gate, and I told my students not to talk as we hiked into the forest. I'm sure that some of them were busy questioning how much else in their lives they were not seeing. After this exercise, at least some students were asking themselves, "What was it in me that kept me from seeing? What are the connections between my own perceptual process and the world around me?"

What indeed! We are accustomed to walking right by the obvious and at the same time are oblivious to the effect we have on our surroundings just by existing. We're not aware of the impact we have with our scent, sound, the way we move, our very presence. The way I teach stalking dissects these impacts, alerting and sensitizing students to the impact we all have on our environment.

A mile into the Quabbin woods I found a good place to sit and I gathered the group around me. It was important that we discussed at some length what we were about to do, because the stalking itself would be done—except for emergencies—in complete silence.

I tell my students what it takes to stalk successfully. These techniques are all part of the meditation of stalking. They pertain to the awareness and quality of attention that bring us into the world of animals and animal perception and so into our own bodies.

One of the things we have to keep in mind in order to stalk successfully is the acute sensitivity of animals' noses. We need to know what the wind is doing, which will determine the direction we're going to walk. We don't want our scent being blown out in front of us, downwind. That way, any animals would know way ahead of time that we're coming. We want the wind in our face, blowing directly at us or across us.

An animal's sense of smell is heightened or curtailed depending on weather conditions. The ideal conditions for an animal to scent you would be when the humidity is twenty to eighty percent, with temperatures between forty to ninety degrees Fahrenheit and ten- to twenty-mile-per-hour breezes. Your best chances for not being detected are in conditions such as rain and falling snow, in a light mist or heavy fog, or in very dry conditions with the humidity below twenty percent, because these conditions interfere with animals' ability to perceive scent.

There are all kinds of things people can do to hide or mask their scent. Some hunters wear rubber boots, for example. Rubber boots don't allow your scent to attach as easily to the ground as do leather boots. But if you leave your rubber boots in your house, they will carry the scent of the house into the forest, alerting wildlife to your presence. Some hunters won't leave their clothes in their houses. They leave them in the woods. If they're working from a blind, they'll leave some of their clothes there to let the animals grow accustomed to their scent.

There is a whole industry that has sprung up to help hunters mask their scent. You can buy the scent of red fox urine. Will deer think that if there's red fox around people can't be around, too? I'm leery of this logic.

You can buy acorn scent. I don't think it smells natural, even though it's the real stuff. It's so removed from the actual environment in which it's supposed to exist, I doubt that it fools wild animals.

Hunters will take deer urine in the snow and rub it on their clothes. This may sound strange, but, surprisingly, deer urine smells great! (I should mention that it is possible in rare instances to pick up diseases from handling animal secretions.) I have experimented with masking scents; if anything, I find they hurt rather than help my chance of seeing wildlife.

I remember one instance, however, when a scent-masking technique did seem to work. I wanted to photograph a red fox den with a litter of young kits. I had seen the kits previously, from quite a way off. Now I wanted to get closer. I knew that if the adults caught my scent they would give the kits an alarm, sending them deep into the den where I'd never see them. So I left my clothes in a dairy barn for days. When I put them on, I smelled like the cows in the barn.

I stalked, getting closer and closer. I came to a crucial distance, perhaps one hundred and fifty to two hundred feet away. I stepped on a big rock, which I thought was going to stay put, but it was balanced on two other rocks. It tilted, lifted up, and came back down with a thud that I knew would definitely carry to the den. I froze, standing perfectly still in camo, drenched in cow scent.

Suddenly, an adult fox walked straight toward me from the direction of the den. Had it heard the noise, come to check it out, smelled cow, and thought it safe to approach? It wasn't until the fox got to within fifteen feet of me that it seemed to realize it was approaching not a cow, but a person!

It stopped dead in its tracks. Its whole facial structure seemed to change. Its eyes got wide while the hairs seemed to stick out more on the side of its face, making the fox look perplexed. It turned and walked away, never looking back. It didn't run.

Overall, I would say masking scents are overrated. I've had six or eight people stalking through the forest who haven't washed in baking soda or left their clothes in a barn and we've still had incredible experiences. Just because you put a masking scent on your body doesn't mean you can hide your scent. Your human scent is still there, and animals can still smell it. Far more important than masking your scent is being aware of how your scent is moving through the forest.

To do this, you must be attentive to the direction of the wind, to the weather, and to the contours of the landscape. You must use wind, weather, and terrain to your advantage. For example, walking in a dried-up creek bed or a little ravine with banks to either side will increase your chances of seeing animals before they see you. This is one of the most secret ways to walk in the forest. Most of your torso is hidden by the banks on either side, but often you'll be able to see into the forest. Scent and sound are deflected by those banks (they function just like sound barriers on a highway). Be aware not only of the direction of wind but also of the terrain around you. Where is your scent going?

Sometimes it's clear which way the wind is blowing. You can feel it on the back of your neck or in your face. Some people will carry a thread about two feet long and hold it up to test the wind. If you can see the breath coming out of your mouth, that's another way to tell wind direction. Then there's the old technique of wetting your finger and holding it up.

Be aware of the terrain around you. Animals use landscape to their advantage. Often deer will lay up on top of a knoll because sound and scent travel up the knoll. They have a view from the knoll or hillsides. You too can use the terrain to your advantage: as you crest the top of a hill, the animals on the other side of the hill might not have heard your approach. One of your best opportunities to see wildlife is to very quietly look out over the top of this crest into the forest in front of you or below you. You have the same opportunity when you come around the corner of a hill or come out from a ravine between two hills. It's the same principle as walking in the dry streambed. The terrain helps you move secretly through the forest.

Besides being aware of your scent when stalking, you must be aware of your sound. Much of the time we walk through our world unaware of the noise we're making and how that noise affects our environment. The chatter in our head drowns out everything else, and we blunder along, deaf to the racket we're making. Imagine that you throw a rock into a still pond, its water like glass. Ripples spread from the place that the rock enters the water. Sound waves are the same. Any noise you make anywhere has a circumference and diameter. It reaches only so far into the forest, as does the noise an animal makes.

You have a perimeter of sound and a perimeter of vision. You can see only so far. If your perimeter of sound as you move through the forest is greater than your perimeter of vision, it's unlikely that you will see any animals before they see you. Keep in mind that if conditions are right, some animals can hear a twig crack hundreds of yards away.

For most people this is what happens. Their perimeter of sound is greater than their perimeter of vision. People often see deer and not other animals because deer often "hold" when they hear you, freezing in their tracks, letting the camouflage of their coats blend into the forest. In most cases, deer would rather hold than run. Freezing is a more effective survival strategy than running, because when a deer runs its senses are clouded, it's making noise, everything is moving. When a deer runs, it exposes itself. When it's still, it may remain unnoticed. This stillness and the camouflage of its coat provide security. A deer is used to people walking right by it. If you get too close, it will bolt. You'll see a white flash of tail and bounding legs as it disappears into the forest. This is how most people see wildlife: the animal running away.

The idea in stalking is to get your perimeter of sound inside your perimeter of vision. If you make a big noise in the woods, you should stop moving. Stop for quite some time. What you've done is send the ripples way out into the forest. When that happens, some animals will stop in their tracks to assess the situation. What was it they heard? They'll sniff the air, trying to get more information. Their ears will be turning, their eyes searching for movement. They may stay in position for a long time. If you move, they're going to zero in on you, and you're not going to see them. You want to wait for them to relax and begin to move again. You have to wait, the longer the better. Then you can start moving again. Alternately, if you've made a loud noise, you could also try to camouflage the sound by imitating the chatter of a squirrel or the rustling it makes when running or foraging in the leaves.

Walking quietly through terrain is an important part of stalking meditation, and it might be a good idea to practice this in your backyard or in a relatively quiet area of a city park before you go out into the woods. One of the first things you want to consider with sound is the ground cover. Are you in a deciduous forest with lots of leaves on the ground? Are the leaves dry? Are there lots of twigs underfoot? Walking in this type of woods will make a racket. When you plan to go stalking, try to wait until the leaves get sopping wet after a heavy rain or fog. A pine or conifer forest is much quieter than a deciduous forest. The needle carpet makes less noise than crinkly leaves.

In winter, the quality of the snow that you're in will also determine how much noise you'll make as you move through the woods. Some snow will crunch or creak. In other snow, however, you can walk almost silently.

Some people go to extremes to walk quietly in the forest. With each foot, they put their toes down first, then the ball of the foot, then they inch down the side of their foot until finally they get to the heel. As with masking scents, I can tell you with confidence that you don't have to go to this extreme in order to see wildlife. You just have to conduct yourself in an appropriate way. You must pay strict attention to where you're putting your feet.

But how can you watch constantly for wildlife and at the same time watch where each and every footstep is going? First, scan the forest to make sure there are no animals in view. Then look down for a place to put your foot. The place should be free of twigs. Actually *look* at this spot. Then go back to watching for wildlife while you lift your foot and place it in the spot you have chosen. Eventually you will be able to choose future steps several at a time.

With practice you will start to be able to "see" with your feet, feeling the ground, the hard and soft places, inserting your feet noiselessly into position. You will be able to find spots for your feet and step into them without actually having to watch where your feet are going. Some people prefer to use moccasins outdoors so they can better feel the ground. You may have problems balancing. As you lift one foot to put it in another place, for a moment you're balanced on one foot. If you lose your balance, the airborne foot will come crashing down. The trick to achieving balance is attention and awareness. If you walk on a railroad track or on any other narrow surface, the way to keep your balance is to actually look at the surface. Focus on every little pit, every mark, every ding in the track's surface. If you're paying attention in that way, your body is getting the information it needs to balance. Then your physical body will take over your thinking self. This can be an exhilarating experience—walking down the railroad track with your body in full control.

Here's an exercise to help you balance. In the woods, your yard, a park, or even in your apartment: focus on something in front of you—a small tree, a branch, a leaf, a light switch, or a door knob. Grab your right ankle with your right hand. Keep looking at whatever it is you're focused on. Really look at it. Don't let your attention wander. Then put your left hand, the one not holding your ankle, straight up into the air. Bend your whole torso forward from the waist up until your left arm is parallel to the ground. Still holding your ankle, try to stretch your right leg straight back.

This posture arches your back and puts a lot of pressure on your right arm. It will be difficult to hold the posture, but staying focused on whatever you're looking at in front of you will help you maintain it. Hold for as long as you can. Then repeat by holding your left ankle.

In addition to balance, it's crucial to understand the human sense of sight and also to have a rough idea of how different animals that we might encounter see the world. Most forest animals have far better hearing than we do and a much better sense of smell. But human vision, especially if we learn how to see in the forest and stay attentive and aware, can compensate for the deficits of our other senses. In some ways our vision may even surpass that of some animals. Some animals don't see color, and they may not see forms as clearly as we do. Deer, like a lot of other mammals, do not see color; they see in shades of gray. We do know that birds see color.

Our thought process also affects how we see things. Our thoughts participate in the act of looking. Thought works by compartmentalizing, dividing up the world into things. When we look at a forest, for example, we see individual objects: trees, a stream, a hill, rocks, birds, animals. We see form. The world is divided up with boundaries, edges, perimeters.

Please excuse what may sound like a presumptuous statement, but I think that I have some idea of the way deer see, and I don't think they see the same way we do. In my experience, deer don't divide, separate, or compartmentalize. You can stand perfectly still right out in the open and a deer may not see you. If you're standing in a fairly open forest and you don't move, and if the deer doesn't catch your scent, it may, eventually, become suspicious of you but it may not actually see you. It may try to call you out (how deer do this is something we'll discuss later in this chapter). But the deer doesn't seem sure whether you're there or not. If you move even a little bit, though, that deer is off. If it catches your scent, it's off.

I think deer smell like we see and we see like deer smell. Let me illustrate what I mean. If you're in your home and you smell a little smoke you might be concerned. You would look around—upstairs, downstairs, room to room. You smell the smoke, or you think you smell it, but you're not sure. Then, suddenly, you see flames. You panic. You run for the fire extinguisher.

The deer has the same response when it sees you. It's concerned. It checks out the situation. But if it *smells* you, it's snorting and it's off. It's gone.

A deer's vision is probably like our peripheral vision. On our periphery we don't really see form. We don't see objects. But if something moves on our periphery that attracts our attention, we turn our heads and focus on that movement, identifying it. You can see the way I think deer see by doing a simple exercise. Take your two index fingers, left and right. Put each one at the periphery of your vision. Then just wiggle them. Try to see both of them at the same time. If you do this you can get to the point where the forest or a city street loses its form, and all you perceive is movement.

I do this when I'm doing long-exposure photography, waiting for plants and trees to stop moving. I change all my vision to peripheral vision so I'm just focused on movement. The forest dissolves into itself and the slightest movement is accented. But turning my vision to peripheral vision is not the mode I use when I'm in the forest looking for wildlife. Mostly what I do is increase the perimeter of my vision, pushing it beyond my sound perimeter.

This is what you want to do when you're stalking: increase the distance you can see into the forest as far as you can. Binoculars will help. You want to move toward open areas in the forest where you can see depth. If an area is too open, however, you will have a hard time hiding yourself. So you want to stalk through a moderately open forest. Ideally, if you can find a transitional zone of thick cover or understory at the edge of more open woodland, then you can keep yourself under cover while looking into more open terrain. Keeping to the shadows and not standing in direct sunlight will also increase your ability to melt into the forest.

I increase my perimeter of vision in the forest by employing what I call pocket vision. The perimeter of vision in the forest is unequal. If you scan in a ninety-degree cone in front of you when you're in the forest, you'll notice that there are some places that you can see quite far (what I call pockets) and other places where undergrowth and the thickness of trees stop your sight line.

I try to focus deep into the forest, but I also make sure to scan the area closer to me first. I keep attuned to movements in the pockets within my perimeter. You can train yourself to detect movement in these pockets—a flicker of a deer's ear, the darting of a fox. Usually you won't see a whole animal, just a part, and most often the animal will be at the edge of the perimeter, not right in front of you. If you become an accomplished stalker, you'll start to see animals closer to you.

There are other ways to increase your perimeter of vision. When you find obstacles in your way, sometimes kneeling down to look beneath them or moving to the side a little will do wonders to increase the distance you can see into the forest.

So now you know that when you're moving through the forest you must be conscious of sound and scent, and you must increase your perimeter of vision. There's one more element that you need to recognize and control as best you can: movement. Movement is your worst enemy in the forest when you're trying to see wildlife. You must be conscious of every movement you make, because each one makes you vulnerable to detection by animals. Try not to grab or brush up against trees or branches in the forest, causing the trees to shake. This will attract animals' attention. Try not to wave at mosquitoes and blackflies. You might as well be waving at the animals, shouting, "I'm over here! I'm over here!" Any little movement, depending on the type of animals around you and their distance from you, will give you away.

Think about what it is to be really still. When you're stalking and you stop, you need to be absolutely still. When you turn your head to look in different directions, turn it slowly. You can move so slowly that it appears you are not moving at all. For example, you see a deer. You want to get your binoculars up to see it. You have choices. If the deer looks away, you can raise your binoculars quickly. But you have to be careful. Deer will trick you. If a deer suspects your presence, it may pretend to lower its head to begin to browse, only to lift it back up quickly in hopes of catching movement. Deer will turn their heads and then quickly turn back. So when you make quick movements you have to be careful not to be seen. There may also be other deer in the area that you don't see, but which will see you when you move and alert the deer you're watching.

If you do think you're being watched, you could move your binoculars slowly up to your eyes. A lot depends on how far away an animal is from you. If it's three hundred feet away, you could probably move your binoculars up slowly, inch by inch. If an animal is only two hundred feet away, you should move much slower, millimeter by millimeter. If the animal is closer than that, forget it. You don't need the binoculars.

I give all my groups of stalking students these instructions and a set of hand signals so that we can communicate in silence. A fist held up means, "I see an animal, freeze." The person who sees the animal looks toward it. An open hand means, "Forget it. Thought I saw something but didn't. Relax."

It took me over an hour to give these instructions to my Quabbin stalkers, and now they are antsy to go. We start off through the woods, walking close together in the manner of Native American hunters who sometimes walked touching each other to disguise their human form. Especially when we stop, I have told the group, we need to close ranks and stay together. I've asked people to either wear camo or dark colors, which helps disguise our human outline.

At first we move relatively quickly, walking for five minutes and then being still for five minutes. I want to get the group away from the area we had first gathered in as quickly as possible. Through our talking and moving around we had disturbed the surroundings. It will take quite a while for that area to forget we were there.

I've chosen to take my students through stands of white pines. The needle floor is soft and quiet, and we move up a hillside, a steady slope. It's steep enough for us to feel ourselves working.

I want to get the group to the top of the hill, away from our disturbed area. But I can't help but notice that on the way up the hill the group is making far too much noise. I call them forward. Little by little, moving slowly they gather around me.

"Please! We have to watch where we're putting our feet," I say. "We have to walk more quietly than we have been. To see an animal before it sees us is no easy thing. We have to take this incredibly seriously. So please be aware of every footstep!"

I lead the group up the hill, keeping them slower this time. We inch up over the crest of the hill and stop. I keep them there for about fifteen minutes. I want the forest to forget us. I want the students to slow down and relax. We go slower and slower and slower, watching what's going on outside of us in the forest and inside of us, with our quality of attention, our awareness, our movement of thought.

I move the group again. We take one step every thirty or sixty seconds. We move this way for five minutes and then stop. We repeat this pattern, walking for five minutes, stopping for ten.

We head into hemlocks. I want to keep to the hemlocks because the needles on the ground will allow us to walk quietly. The group has been very quiet, very conscious, their feet whispering along the ground. They're looking around in all different directions. Suddenly, I feel a nudge from the person behind me. I slowly turn my head to see where he's looking. There's a deer coming toward us. My student is in a state of high excitement. He's not sure that I've seen the deer so he slaps me lightly on the back to alert me. The deer bolts off.

The deer didn't snort a warning, so the incident should not have penetrated too far into the forest. I hold the group still for fifteen minutes. We start to move again, slowly through the hemlock. Sometimes we have to duck way down to get underneath low dead branches. We can see quite a distance through the forest. The day is dark, cloudy, and still, a good day for spotting deer. Deer tend not to move when it's windy, perhaps because they become disoriented when the forest is pitching about in an uproar.

When we stop, far into the forest's depths, I think I see movement. I'm looking through a dark tunnel into a bright spot, perhaps two hundred yards distant, and there I see the silhouette of a deer's leg.

I put my fist up. I don't think this deer can see me. There's no movement. I raise my binoculars with one hand to my eyes. Sure enough, it's a deer. I can clearly see its leg and part of its torso.

The only thing to do now is wait. This deer has probably not seen us, so we have the upper hand. From here on it's luck. It could move toward us or away from us. We may never see more than one leg. Suddenly, I can't see the leg anymore. But I keep the group still.

It's a really good group. They hold tight. I see more movement. A doe is coming toward us. Then I see another one and another and another. Four does are picking their way through the forest, browsing every now and then, cautiously stopping, moving with fits and starts but steadily and slowly approaching.

I can feel the wind lightly puffing against my right cheek. This appears to be good, until I realize the wind is shifting. I can feel it moving around my cheek and neck and on to my back.

The group is tight and still. The deer are heading directly toward us. Will they pick up our scent? They stop, ruffled, nostrils flaring. Their heads are up, alert. They've caught a whiff of us, but they don't know where our scent is coming from.

Now the deer won't move. They've detected danger but they don't know where it is. They're in a tight group; their torsos mostly point toward us, but they're all looking in different directions. This is common for a group of deer when they're on alert.

We stand frozen for ten minutes in a stalemate. We wait. Another ten minutes. The wind shifts again. I feel it on my cheek. The deer relax. They haven't caught another scent of us. But they don't seem to want to proceed in our direction. They move off to our left into a heavy cover of hemlocks. We lose sight of them.

I wait another five minutes. This is a long time to keep people perfectly still. I can sense the tension and the strain. I hear their breath. I can almost hear their joints creak as they try to imperceptibly shift their weight from one foot to the other, taking the strain off their necks and lower backs.

I'm just about to start everyone forward when I detect more movement in front of us. I look and I just can't be happier for these people. It's unbelievable. A buck is coming right at us, on the same path as the four does.

The deer is thick in the neck, with a tawny brown coat and a magnificent spread of curving antlers. He looks immensely powerful. He stops at about the same place as the does did.

The air is still now—still and cold and little bit heavy. It's overcast, late in the afternoon in the deep green of the hemlock grove. I can feel the accelerated beat of my students' hearts as the buck stops.

Nobody's moving. Not a hair. No one dares pick up their binoculars. The buck is suspicious, the moment is tense. He walks closer to us, stops, bends his head down to the ground as though he's going to eat something, then picks it up fast. He stomps his foot on the ground, as if to call us out. He stomps again, and waits.

We're very close together, in a huddle. We don't look like a human being, and he doesn't seem to know what we are. He circles around, arcing away from us, and we lose sight of him. The group has been standing still for over forty minutes. I can feel that, breathless and excited as they are, they're close to collapse. How much longer will they be able to contain themselves? But I keep them silent, still, waiting. I know that deer sometimes come back. They seem to be curious animals.

And that's just what this buck does. He comes even closer to us this time to within one hundred seventy-five feet. He stops, looks at us for several minutes, then puts his head down. His great rack of antlers extends out in front of him, and he makes a bluff charge. He runs directly at us, head down. He stops short, quickly lifts his head and looks at us. We don't move, standing there unhinged, agape.

Finally, the buck moves off. I figure he's got to be gone. I let my students relax. They can't believe what they've just seen. They're elated, pumped up, but I tell them to be quiet and move slowly. They cautiously gather themselves to get going again, when I catch the buck coming at us from a new direction! He still hadn't scented us.

I put my fist up again, quickly, and everybody freezes. They can't believe their eyes. This buck is coming in for another look. This time he's approaching from behind us (deer will often circle around and approach you from behind). Finally, he catches our scent. He leaps to one side, charging into the woods, snorting.

The group has a snack, still in complete silence. With an hour of daylight left, it's time to start moving out of the forest. The hike out is a couple of miles, much of it uphill. The cloud cover is thick now, low and gray. It may snow. I want to move the group out of the darkness of the conifers into a lighter area for our closing ritual: a call to the coyotes.

I lead the group to a knoll overlooking some fields. Across the fields and up in the hills live a family of coyotes that has bred there for years. I ask everybody to be quiet and still when we get to the top of the knoll.

When I do this ritual I stand for five minutes in meditation. I envision the coyote packs, and I think of coyotes that I've seen. I want to get a good picture of them in my head before I howl. I ask for their help.

It's an adult coyote howl that I do. It sounds like a siren. It starts off slow with a whine that eventually breaks and then goes back to a whine. I end with some yipping. As I finish my howl a whole family group of coyotes starts yipping and howling and yipping and howling from the hills across the field. I howl again and they respond. The third time I howl they're silent. In my experience, they seldom answer more than twice.

Now we really have to get back to the parking area. I take the group on a shortcut, on a logging road across a cove forested with big white pines. We trace a path through the pinewood that skirts the water's edge. Quabbin Reservoir's small waves lap under a low gray sky. The air is chilly, smelling of pine sap and deep water.

The coyotes howl again, stopping us in our tracks. It sounds as though they've come to the knoll where we had been howling at them. We all howl back at them this time, but they don't answer. After hiking another quarter of a mile, we hear the coyotes howling again, from the cove where we had just been. They were tracking us. We come out of the woods in the last light as it starts to snow.

The experience of the group that day in Quabbin was about being present, alive, awake in the moment. It was about being aware. This kind of awareness brings clarity to our lives. Learning to be attentive in the forest, aware of our presence, opens us to intimacy with the movements of animals in the outer landscape and the movement of thought, which is the trail of the self in our inner landscape.

From my perspective, the most important thing that the great philosopher Krishnamurti said was "Pay attention!" Everything we ever need to learn, if we want to know deeply who we are, if we want to know what keeps us from connecting with nature, is all here in front of us all the time. All we have to do is pay attention, be aware.

This awareness can be present whether talking to a friend, splitting wood, or driving a car. It's a quality of attention, of living from moment to moment. It is the quality of attention of the deer we saw in Quabbin, ears catching every sound, eyes picking up every movement, nose inspecting every waft of air. Those animals were totally immersed in their senses. They were alive, awake, sensitive. They embraced their surroundings with their whole beings.

Oftentimes we're not living that quality of attention of that wild animal in the forest. We live complex lives that call for thought and decision-making all the time. We juggle work and family. Many of us have highly technical jobs that demand that we utilize thought intensively. Our world seems to be moving increasingly in this direction. It's easy to see that thought is important, but we must also be able to see its limitations.

We human beings have become very distracted, in many different ways. Probably our biggest distraction is the thought process itself. The thought process is an incredible tool for survival. As we look around, we see the results of human thought everywhere. Computers, a chair, a house, boat, car—the list is endless. The children of thought surround us. We live among them and with them and through them.

Thought has taken over our lives in more ways than we can even begin to imagine. In order for awareness to enter our lives, we need to understand how thought envelops us, permeates us, and controls us. It is the thought process that is in large part responsible for keeping us from connecting with nature, the outer landscape, and our own nature—the wild within.

Stalking is a marvelous way to begin to explore what keeps us disconnected from the inner and outer landscapes. There is an inner chatter and an image of ourselves that thought has created and to which we have become vitally attached, keeping us from the connection and communion that so many of us feel lacking in our lives. Stalking creates an opportunity to learn about our fragmentation. It's about how we look and listen.

What have we lost with this ascendance of thought in our lives and in our world? I am not advocating primitivism, or a return to nature, though I often think that might not be such a bad idea. Even though I live way out in the woods, my own life is technology-driven. I am tied to phones, computers, cars, e-mail, and fax.

But all of our man-made environment, our technological products of thought, distract us and separate us from who we really are. You might be walking down a city street and not really see one single person passing you. I think one of the things that makes it difficult to pay attention in cities is the overload of stimulation, the prevalence of the products of thought all around that tend to confirm thought's ascendance, its sense of supremacy, and its self-importance. This is one of the reasons I think it's important to experience the silence of the forest.

Thought can also intrude when you're walking in the woods. Say you're walking through a tamarack bog, sphagnum moss at your feet, a trail cutting through it. There's a tremendous amount of moisture in the air. The air is thick. There's not a whisper of wind. It's incredibly quiet. There's the smell of conifers, juniper, and cedar. Birds in the canopy twitter and flit.

You're hiking through this forest at a leisurely pace. But ten or fifteen minutes later, you realize that the forest has changed. Now you're in an upland forest of ash, oak, and hickory. The smells are completely different. The ground is dry and rocky. There's no moss.

You didn't notice the transition. You look back down the trail. You don't see any conifers. You didn't notice the change. You realize you were talking to yourself about something, thinking about something. And you can't remember what it was you were talking or thinking about.

Where are we half the time? We're walking in a daze. We're asleep, not awake. We're not present. Why? Why are we not living the moment? The thought process has taken over to the point where we're not even aware of the fact that it has done so.

One of the ways thought dulls us is by making us think we're looking when we're not. This is what happened in the beginning of my stalking program, when my students thought they were looking for their instructor who was right next to them. But unconsciously they had already made the decision that I wouldn't be where I was. The thought process predisposed them to not seeing me.

Stalking meditation demands that we pay full attention to every footfall, every breath, every sound we make, each nuance of landscape, wind, humidity. Stalking gives us an opportunity to move away from the tiny perspective of thought and self into an all-encompassing awareness. When we are in this awareness we see with the eyes of the whole universe. The tiny perspective of self is put in its place, seen for what it is. It is no longer a frightened little identity hiding in a vast wilderness.

The quality of attention that we're talking about here is not only the quality of attention of the tracker in the forest, but the quality of attention of the coyote watching the deer graze and the deer eyeing the coyote, of the eagle soaring high overhead, and the fisher stashing its food under the snow. It is the fox that comes to investigate the thud of the rock near its den and the buck charging with its antlers low to the ground. It is the coyotes calling from the cove as evening comes and the first snow falls. It is your body moving silently, slowly in the gathering dark. It is the wild within.

5.

THE TERRITORY

OF SELF

For many animals, scent is an important tool for identifying themselves and marking their territory. We humans have territorial behaviors as well, and in this chapter we'll explore the ways in which our valid need for personal space has become entwined with our psychological needs to feel important, dominant, and secure.

To understand the world of animal scent, one of the first things we need to be clear about is just how much more sensitive some animals' noses are than our own. An average person has five million olfactory cells. With 220 million olfactory cells, a sheepdog can smell 44 times better than we can. A bloodhound can follow a track that is over two weeks old. It can pick up the scent of a person in a room that person left hours ago, and then distinguish that person's scent from others. Using their noses, deer and squirrels can find food under a foot of snow. A bear can smell you from a mile away, and it can smell a carcass from several miles.

Let's look at what happens with scent molecules when they enter our nasal cavity. It's important to realize that these molecules are the real stuff of the thing we are smelling. If you are smelling beaver cas-toreum (a secretion from the beaver's scent gland), what you recog-nize as a scent are actually small particles of the beaver that have entered your body. These particles, thousands of them, come in con-tact with neurons in the upper back of your nasal cavity. Your body has just grabbed on to a beaver!

You're having what I call a direct experience. This does not mean that the inner thought process you are always having inside your head won't step in. You may say rationally, "I am smelling beaver." But this is not the same as the actual *experience* of smelling beaver. When we look at a tree or a person we often experience our *idea* about that ob-ject or person, not the object itself. In other words, we don't embrace things with all our senses, with our whole being. We live too much in our heads, causing our ideas to get in the way of direct sensory expe-rience.

Try this simple exercise:

Close your eyes and picture the color red. You can "see" it in your mind's eye, but what you're "seeing" is your idea or image of the color red, which is the residue of actual direct sensory experience. It is not the same, however, as the sensory experience of actually seeing red. Now picture a hemlock. You have an idea of it in your head, but it is not the direct sensory experience of seeing a hemlock.

The idea or image I have of an object can dilute and obscure the full sensory experience of it. When I look into the forest and say, "That's a red oak tree, that's a beech," I recognize and label those trees. This takes very little information, just enough to fit my idea of the trees. But I didn't participate fully in the direct sensory act of looking at them. If I had, I would have noticed the tree frog clinging to the trunk of the oak, or the fresh bear claw marks on the beech, or hundreds of other fascinating details. Recognition and identification need to happen, but when they start to replace direct seeing—when I just label and then don't go on to *see* what I've labeled—I'm no longer experiencing life fully, with my whole being.

John Seed, forest activist, coauthor of *Thinking Like a Mountain*, and cofounder of The Council of All Beings, once showed me an interesting process that dramatically demonstrated how removed from our senses we can be. On a fourteen-by-twenty-inch chart he had painted the words *yellow, black, blue, red, green, orange,* and *brown.* The words were not painted in the same color as the color the word represented: that is, the word *red* was painted in yellow and the word *green* was painted in red, etc.

Holding up this chart, he asked people to quickly say the colors the words were painted, not the words themselves. There was a group of about fifteen of us and hardly anyone could do it. He held it upside down, and many people still found themselves saying the word rather than the color. This exercise dramatically demonstrates how caught up our visual process is with thought. We focused on the thought process of the name of the color, not on the sensory experience of seeing colors themselves. It's no wonder that we look at a tree, say it's a hemlock and think we actually see it, but don't. This is why we often don't really see what we are looking at.

Humans are visual creatures and so it's hard for us to grasp the complexity and magnitude of information available to animals who depend on senses other than vision. I've developed an exercise to help my tracking students understand how information comes to animals through scent. This Scent Visualization Exercise can be done anywhere.

Imagine you're sitting in a chair in a room. Try to visualize the scent coming off your body. Think about what that scent is. It's particles of you—who you are. It's molecules of your very essence. Sitting in a room, your scent is coming off you continually. Imagine your scent is colored. Pick a color that appeals to you and seems to represent your scent. I'll use purple here.

Scent seeps from your body. Soon the room in which you sit is filled with the color of your scent: a purple glow clings to your chair. Scent glows like an aura around you. It drifts into the far corners of the room, seeps under the door, and glides in wisps and little glowing particles through connected rooms and hallways.

Now take that same model and apply it in nature. Visualize yourself walking down a path in the forest and then standing still in a woodland glade. It's an unusually warm sunny afternoon in early fall, a season rich with new smells. The glade is carpeted with long grass and scattered white pines. Stand with your arms at your side. Relax. Breathe in the fullness of the coming autumn, taking deep breaths, in and out, drawing the warm air in through your nose, into your lungs and diaphragm, then slowly expelling it through your nose. Keep breathing, slowly and deeply. Close your eyes and feel the warmth of the sun on your skin.

Pick out smells in the glade: the warm grass, the rich warm earth. Notice different types of plant fragrances: the grass-like smell of ferns, the calming odor of conifers, the fruity smell of ripe wild grapes. Visualize your own purple scent wafting from your body into the glade. It curls into the forest, traveling like pollen on streams of air. In the forest, hidden from you, are animals—foxes, rabbits, woodchucks, deer, bobcat, coyotes, field mice. Colored scent, a different color for each species, is oozing from all of them, swirling through the air in streams.

Look back down the path you took to enter the glade. You can see the color of your scent trail. There are purple blotches everywhere you stepped. Visualize your scent clinging to the grasses and branches you may have rubbed against. The longer you stay in one spot, the deeper purple that area appears as it takes on your color. The whole forest is a kaleidoscope of color, filled with different scents and rich with information about all who have passed here. You can see where a deer walked and lingered by the grapevines. Vole trails are everywhere—ribbons of color cutting and winding through the wet parts of the glade. You can see where a fox has come to hunt the voles. By visualizing scents, we can gain an understanding of what some animals can "see" with their noses. In the same way that we see, animals smell. Their sense of smell is that clear, that defined.

Not only do animals have scent information available to them, they are also constantly and purposefully giving and receiving information through the use of their olfactory organs. Using scent, they shout to the far reaches of the forest:

"I am!"

"My place."

"Where are you?"

"I'm over here."

"It's mating time."

"Keep out—private!"

And much, much more.

Animals send these signals by depositing scent through glands. Canines, felines, mustelids, and others have scent glands in their anuses that add various odors to their scat. These animals, plus deer, also have scent glands in their hooves and paws, which deposit scent wherever they go. This is in addition to the body scent they leave just by their passing. Some animals also have a distinctive scent to their urine, which varies depending on whether it's mating season or not.

The location in which animals deposit their scent is often significant. Canines, including foxes and coyotes, will typically deposit their scat in the middle of a trail or on top of an elevated rock. It's as if they're trying to make sure it doesn't go unnoticed. Bears will defecate in the middle of roads, announcing themselves boldly. Fox, coyote, and bear are all saying "I am!" with their scat. They are proclaiming themselves with their essence, an odor that communicates their existence and individuality with an undeniable immediacy.

When it comes to the world of animal scent, the beaver is the premier exhibitionist, building showy scent mounds and infusing them with a remarkably potent odor. You can smell a fresh beaver scent mound from thirty feet away. I've often felt compelled to stand at attention and salute, or at least give a little bow, when I've come into a beaver's territory and smelled one of these mounds. It's the beavers' intention to make known their presence, and there's no doubt they do the job well.

Beavers scent their mounds with castoreum. The mounds sometimes reach two feet high and are made from decaying leaves, conifer needles, twigs, and mud. Beavers will utilize any debris under the water at a pond's edge. They don't seem to be fussy. They pick up this material with their front paws, much like a person would, then walk upright onto the water's bank on their hind feet. The beavers traverse the mound, depositing castoreum from their castor gland on its top. The castor gland is located just beneath the skin anterior to the cloacal opening, which is where the beaver's genitals and anus are.

Let me tell you about an experience that a friend, whom I'll call Spud, had in the wilderness of northern Maine. Spud often goes off-trail to places where very few people have ventured. In one such place he found a beaver colony far from human contact; one spring, he spent two weeks hanging out with those beavers. The beavers began to accept him, coming right up to him, taking poplar branches from his hand and sitting down next to him to eat them.

The beaver family that Spud observed consisted of two adults. One was a very large, old, crusty, mean-looking beaver, who even appeared to have gray hair. He had a fierce demeanor, but he would eat from Spud's hand just like the other beavers. There were two small babies from the year's spring litter and an older sibling from the previous year. It was a typical beaver family. The juveniles stayed along shore near the lodge, cruising back and forth, lolling about, just hanging out and relaxing, while the big male beaver industriously pulled large branches from the woods, dragging them and paddling them back across the pond to the lodge. Each time the male returned to the vicinity of the lodge, the juveniles squeaked greetings and clamored around the grizzled patriarch, who paid them no attention, but went on diligently about his business. At exactly 2:15 each afternoon, for half an hour, the female beaver would gather sticks and pawfuls of mud and place them on the lodge. Walking erect on her hind feet, she would carry the mud and sticks in her paws. Spud tried this mud-carrying technique, and he found that the mud alone was quite heavy and that it took both strength and coordination to carry it and the sticks at the same time.

When Spud returned home from the wilderness, he told me and a trapper friend, Charlie, about the extraordinary relationship he had developed with the Maine beavers. Charlie was intrigued. The next time he saw Spud he brought him a vial of castoreum from a beaver he had trapped and suggested that Spud test the Maine beavers' reactions to the scent. I was concerned about this plan, which I felt was an unfair intrusion into the life of these beavers, disruptive and manipulative. But Spud was curious and took the vial of castoreum on his next trip to Maine, which took place in the fall.

Spud hiked into a rugged low-lying area of bogs and meadows, mixed hardwood and spruce forest. A gorge ran down between two mountains, and the brook at its bottom was marked with beaver sign—old dams, cuttings, and scent mounds. He bushwhacked to the pond where he had observed the beavers during the spring. Lo and behold, there they were, going about their business, living their beaver lives. They seemed to recognize Spud. When he first arrived, they were nervous, slapping the water with their tails, diving into the pond and disappearing. But he started talking to them, in the same cadence he had the previous spring, reassuring them and telling them what lovely animals they were. The beavers calmed down. Spud cut poplar boughs and spread them on the ground near him. The beavers came over and began to feed. Spud and the beavers fell into their old relationship. When he arrived at the pond each morning, the beavers came round him and waited for him to begin gathering poplar branches, which they'd take from his hands.

On the last day of his trip, Spud decided to experiment with Charlie's little vial of castoreum. Spud cut a thin twig, the size and shape of a lollipop handle, and dipped it into the vial. As he removed the stick, the tiniest drop of castoreum shook loose and spattered his finger. He stuck the stick in the side of the dam the beavers had built and retreated to a distance of twenty yards.

Almost immediately all the beavers came out of the lodge. The big crusty male beaver came out first, frantically slapping his tail against the water. Then he began walking up and down on the dam, hissing. The other beavers followed, slapping their tails on the water, continually hissing without, it seemed, any need to breathe. They tore the dam apart on the spot where Spud had deposited the castoreum. They seem to be looking frantically around for the beaver who left it. Then they found Spud.

Those beavers didn't look too friendly as they came hissing and spitting toward him. That big, old, crusty, mean-looking beaver looked meaner than ever. He came right up to Spud, a foot and a half away, hissing into his face. Spud placed his finger marked with the offending drop of castoreum under his armpit to try to mask the scent. But the big beaver was spitting at Spud, standing right between his legs. Spud began talking to him in a soft monotone, saying, "nice beaver, good beaver." The beaver seemed to recognize him and calm down.

Spud felt sorry that he had agitated the beavers and felt as though he had violated their trust. He left Maine the next day. When he returned to the lodge the following spring, the water level in the creek and pond had dropped about three feet, and the lodge was deserted. The beavers had moved on.

Looking at this incident, it seems clear that the beavers were outraged that another beaver had the audacity to come into their territory and leave a territorial marker—as though this was an unthinkable act. Maybe it's how you would feel if you came home one day to find that someone you'd never heard of had graffitied the walls of your home with his name. Most of us would, like the beavers, be frightened and angry.

Through these scent-marking examples, we can clearly see the link between territoriality and the expression of individuality and self in the animal kingdom. Beginning with the publication of Robert Ardrey's 1966 book of popular science, *The Territorial Imperative,* much has been written in recent years about our own biological impulse toward territoriality. It is generally conceded in the scientific community that man shares many of the territorial urges of animals and that notions of private property, statehood, and nationalism may have their origin in our biological makeup.

What isn't as clear is how *ideas* seem to become grafted on top of these biological urges, so that ideas, which are an extension of what I call the territory of the self, take up so much space in our world and are upheld with the same vigorous displays of aggressive behavior that animals exhibit in defending their territory. For example, in my motorcycle days my idea of myself as a leader would, if questioned by one of the gang members, lead me to a territorial display—an act of aggression like flipping a finger at him and saying, "Screw you, Jack!"

If animals mark their territory and proclaim their individuality through scent, how do we, as humans, display individuality and territoriality? We use visual symbols: flags, fences, no trespassing signs, uniforms, graffiti, you name it.

Painting graffiti was one of the ways in which the gangs I led expressed territoriality. When I reentered nature after my gang days, I was struck with the similarities between how animals use scat and scent to mark territory and how we humans use graffiti.

Look at the most basic kind of graffiti: JOE WAS HERE. What is that all about? There's a powerful urge in some people to proclaim themselves in this way. Sometimes you'll see JOE crossed out and FRANK written over it. Wherever Davy Crockett and Daniel Boone went, from Virginia to the Ohio Valley, they carved their names in trees, affirming their existence as they traversed what at that time was the wild immensity of the Appalachian woodlands. This is the same kind of statement we make when planting a flag on the moon or on Everest's summit.

What is this behavior about? I know that for me and my gangs, graffiti was a way of announcing ourselves. Gang graffiti is not only a territorial announcement of *place.* It also confirms and even celebrates the fact that the *gang exists*. This may sound funny, but think about where you see most graffiti. Well-traveled areas: highways, subway stations, and, of course, bathrooms. Where people travel, defecate, and urinate, there seems to be an irresistible urge to mark with graffiti. How ancient!

One hot, hazy July day, working as a loon warden for the Metropolitan District Commission, I sat on one of thousands of boulders that dot the shoreline of Quabbin Reservoir, watching a pair of loons through binoculars. I lunched on the boulder and took notes throughout the afternoon. When I came back the next day to continue my observation, there, right on the exact same spot where I'd been sitting the day before, was coyote scat.

The coyote had gone out of its way to defecate right where I had placed my butt. Sitting there all day, with my own scent oozing from my pores, I might as well have also defecated on that rock. In coyote terms, REZENDES WAS HERE was written in screaming letters. Coyote had made a big X across my marks and written instead, COYOTE WAS HERE.

This type of scent marking crosses species lines. Wolves defecate on traps, poisoned bait, and even beer cans! Why? Perhaps to warn younger animals of danger, or express dominance, even disdain or contempt, for the humans who are trying to entrap them or despoil their habitat. I've found a small weasel scat on top of a big coyote scat. Foxes go out of their way to defecate and urinate on muskrat lodges, or at an entrance to another animal's den, like a woodchuck hole. I have heard that long ago Native Americans would sneak into an enemy's camp and defecate, expressing disdain, scorn, and bravery. Imagine stepping out of your lodge barefoot into shit. That must have been a powerful and very direct way to say many things at once! It's the kind of statement that cuts through thought to our core.

Scientists now think that territorial markings to warn off intruders may be secondary to territorial mapping for the benefit of the home pack, and especially for younger animals. An alpha wolf on the move may scent mark or inspect a scent mark once every two minutes. These marks may help other wolves locate kill sites and productive hunting areas, and even communicate information on pack members' health and mood—whether the wolves are, say, relaxed, fearful, or aggressive.

Scent, in the form of pheromones, plays an integral part in the mating rituals of many mammals. *Pheromone* comes from two Greek words: *pherein,* to carry, and *horman,* to excite. During moose breeding season, I've observed moose pheromones in action. In certain areas, it's common to see a bull following a cow around wherever she goes. The bull tries to get closer and closer to the cow, his nose reaching for her genital area until he gets a good sniff. This has a visible effect. His head extends forward and up and his lips curl back. Occasionally this display will be followed by the bull's attempt to mate.

Male voles will run around making as many urine/scent deposits as possible. They will continually try to cover each other's scent. On any given site, there will be layer upon layer of scent from different voles. The vole able to cover every, or almost every, other scent is the one with the best chance of mating. Female voles are attracted to the smell on top, the most dominant smell. Talk about advertising and name recognition! These dominant male voles would probably make good politicians—the one who ends up the most famous wins the election.

A lot of us humans seek fame and name recognition too. Look at the fuss we make over celebrities. We crave that feeling of being on top of the world, everyone clapping and making a fuss over us. And if we're not succeeding in being famous, maybe notorious will do. Gang or government leader, graffiti or campaign slogan, there's often not much difference in our need for recognition.

Many animals are territorial because they have to be. They require physical space in order to meet their need for food, cover, and to raise their young. People, too, need space to meet our needs. But people differ from most animals when we go beyond our basic needs. Some people have far more than they need while others are impoverished. A multibillionaire builds a $40 million home, while a stone's throw away, the homeless huddle in cardboard boxes.

When our world was populated with small bands or tribes vying for territory and we fought with spears, and bows and arrows, our territorial behavior didn't threaten our existence as a species. But now that we wield weapons of mass destruction, much of our territorial behavior is no longer appropriate. Territorial displays with atomic bombs can wipe out thousands, perhaps millions, of people in an instant.

From my gang days, I know that, in addition to an appropriate desire for physical space to fulfill our basic human needs, we are also driven to claim inner territory. As a motorcycle gang leader I had to project a macho persona, which was expressed in the way I dressed, acted, combed my hair, carried myself, smoked my stogie, and talked street slang. This persona reflected ideas I had about myself: tough, adventurous, fearless, the leader of the pack. These ideas take up inner space, and emotions like pride, fear, and desire become attached to them. This inner territory has to be protected, defended, fortified, and, in my case, projected outward by the creation of a following, which was my gang. The territory of self claimed more and more space inside me and more and more space in the world until it almost destroyed me. It almost landed me in prison and came close to getting me killed.

When the territory of self starts to expand, with it comes a feeling of power and dominance. Being the leader of a gang, a powerful lawyer, a famous actor, artist, expert tracker—being looked up to, admired, feared—gives us a feeling of expansion. We are all familiar with the expressions "he's got a big head" and "he's full of himself." This is the territory of self—it feeds and grows on the admiration, adulation, or fear of others.

Self claims territory not only within itself but also in others. If I become a follower, or if I'm afraid of or being dominated by someone, that person has claimed territory in me and I have allowed it to happen. Some people are very good at claiming territory. Those who are able to expand their territory into other people's lives have an incredible sense of power, supremacy, and dominance.

I knew this feeling as the alpha biker in my gang. When I walked into a bar with my gang strung out behind me, the room would grow silent, everyone's head would turn, and then they would quickly look at the floor. I'd see their shoulders slump and watch how they contracted themselves into submissive postures. If I had been a wolf, I would have smelled fear coming off their bodies. Our gang claimed the area of Fall River, Massachusetts, and no one in their right minds would have started a rival motorcycle gang on our turf or tried to muscle in on our territory.

One of the ways we marked our territory was through graffiti. We left it wherever we went, writing DDMC, which stood for Devil's Disciples Motorcycle Club. We left it in public places to indicate to the world that this was our territory. We proclaimed our identity and our territory with other visual cues too, in much the same way as animals proclaim themselves with scent. Our club patch (our emblem, or colors) was extremely important to all members of the gang. Sewn to the back of our denim jackets, the emblem was worn religiously and was treated with the highest honor. One of the worst things that could possibly happen would be for a rival gang—in a fight or through theft—to get your colors. You were expected to protect them with your life.

At its root, the identification of a gang with its colors, graffiti, and emblems is not different from nationalism with its graffiti and colors. Instead of DDMC, it might be USA. We wear uniforms, pledge allegiance to the flag in school, and espouse the ideas of democracy and capitalism as though these are God-given truths. We proudly proclaim our identity as Americans. The ideals may be different, but the attachment, pride, honor, and need to belong to something powerful is the same.

What was it we were protecting as a gang? I know that as a gang leader I was defending psychological space that was an extension of my image of my self. The self was establishing its identity and territory. The gang was its extension. It was putting up boundaries, fences, walls, waging wars with other gangs, mounting a defense of its honor. On the one hand, the self garnered a tremendous amount of pleasure from its sense of power and supremacy, from its acceptance within its chosen world. But, on the other hand, if my pride was injured or my power questioned, I experienced fear and insecurity. My image of self was subject to tremendous suffering, which the self tried to repress or disavow.

Our lives are manipulated by the self and its territorial behavior. Self reacts in the same way as a fox I tracked on a clear cold winter day in the hilly terrain of Bearsden Conservation Area in northcentral Massachusetts. The fox was going along its merry way, leaving an occasional dab of urine on a prominent object on the trail, such as a shrub, rock, or stump. But then it came to a fisher's trail, fresh in the snow. The fox scratched and urinated over the fisher's scent, giving the fisher's trail a notable amount of attention. It's unusual for the fox to go to this length with another species, even when it crosses a coyote's trail, since the coyote could be a potential threat to the fox. In that case, the fox might change its course a little to inspect the trail, but it is soon on its way again.

Because I was familiar with this particular area and the location of the fox's den, I knew that the fisher was moving through the heart of the fox's home range. This area is the fox's home, its birthing place, its main source of food, water, and cover. Wherever the fox goes in this territory, it comes in contact with its own scent. This may be reassuring in some way to the fox's sense of place, like a biker coming across his own graffiti or gang colors.

The fisher is a member of the weasel family, a powerful predator, seemingly with boundless energy, capable of killing animals larger than itself. This fox was making a tremendous fuss over this particular fisher, so I couldn't help but think that the fox felt threatened in some way. Scenting the fisher's trail may have helped the fox reassert its sense of territorial domination and control. My gang would have responded in a similar way to another gang's name that appeared near our clubhouse by immediately painting over it.

Our human sense of self can be threatened in much the same way that the fox was threatened by the fisher. If self perceives a threat, it vigorously attempts to damage, remove, or supplant the threat, or it throws up all kinds of defenses. It is one of the sad ironies of our world that the bigger the territory the self claims, the more threats it perceives, as other selves compete for territory and the more defenses it throws up. Someone insults our country, religion, or gang, or burns our flag, and we're ready to kill over it. This is an extreme example of what can happen, but it does happen. Whatever pride wraps itself around, it claims as territory. It is pride that makes graffiti.

I had known that I wanted to leave the gang world for some time. I was afraid that I might have to order someone physically harmed, or worse, and the violence and brutality of my life had become abhorrent. But leaving the gang was not so easy. I'd pledged my allegiance, my very life, to my *compadres*. I'd been involved with them in various illegal activities. I'd been a leader. Leaving the gang felt like what I imagine it must feel like to try to leave the Mafia: you'd better have an iron-clad reason.

I eventually had that reason but not without grave danger and almost an immense personal cost. One night, I was home asleep when I heard men storming up the stairs. I thought it was the Gypsy Jokers, a rival motorcycle gang, come to make trouble. I had a lot of guns lying around the house. I jumped out of bed, bare-ass naked, and went for my pistol in the drawer of my night table. My intention was to fire a few rounds into the ceiling to give the Jokers pause. Before I reached the gun, in burst policemen in flak jackets, revolvers drawn.

"State Police Narcotics Bureau. Freeze! You're under arrest!"

Can you imagine what would have happened if they had burst in one second later and found me with my gun in hand? I probably would have been shot. In that moment, my life was hanging by a thread.

It was a tense, gut-wrenching scene. The police tore the place apart, finding three shopping bags full of marijuana and an illegal weapon that was eventually added to the drug charges brought against me and my wife. My kids were wailing, the baby and the three-year-old. We called my brother to come and get them as my wife and I were carted off to jail.

I'll never forget standing before the judge for sentencing, my wife standing at my side. "I sentence you to five to ten years in Walpole State Prison," he said. At that moment it felt as though my whole life had come apart at the seams. This wasn't who I saw myself as—a convict, a felon, living behind bars, losing a large chunk of my youth, separated from my family and friends. I had an inkling at the time that this was where the self's gluttonous need for territory—its thirst for dominance and acceptance—had led. But, as it turned out, it took me many more years to fully understand the lesson life was teaching me.

After my sentence was announced, I was stunned. It seemed to me an eternity before I heard the judge say, "Sentence suspended." I have always wondered how much time actually elapsed. Both my wife and I were given probation, and I now had the perfect excuse to leave the gang. The other members would understand that I had to lay low.

I spent the next several years in a fervent spiritual search. I hadn't yet realized that the territory of self had simply transferred itself from being an alpha biker to a spiritual savant. I reentered the woods and began to synthesize the lessons of nature and spirituality that would direct the rest of my life. Finally, walking in the woods, I had a moment of insight that exploded the notion of self that I had been carrying and cultivating all those years. I realized that the problem is that we really are not able to see the problem. We think we see, but we are not seeing directly. We don't see it in the way that we experience smelling beaver castoreum, or seeing the color red, just like we may not really see a tree when we simply take note that it is a hemlock. Our intellects end up *labeling* the problem—self, territoriality, overpopulation, a behavior problem—and we think we understand it.

But we don't see it directly enough, deeply enough for it to change our behavior. Only real understanding—direct seeing—brings change. Labeling the problem is like telling a two-year-old, "The stove is hot. Don't touch it." The child may understand that it's bad to touch the stove, but when she experiences what hot *is* the words take on a whole new dimension of meaning, and the child's behavior changes. Labeling creates no real change until we fully, directly experience the self.

6.

SHARING

THE PATH

I HAD BEEN IN BAXTER STATE PARK FOR SEVERAL DAYS one October, staying at Roaring Brook Campground. I shared a lean-to with my friend Bill Byrne, and my friends Bill Fournier and Mark Picard shared another lean-to. Baxter is one of my favorite places in the Northeast, and probably the best place for observing moose.

Hunting in most parts of Baxter has been outlawed since the early part of the century, and the moose are generally unafraid of people. You can get quite close to them, although this is not recommended. Moose can behave unpredictably, especially during the fall mating season. I had been shooting photos of moose for my stock photography business, adding to my store of knowledge about moose behavior and habitat and just hanging out with them.

Contact with my friends was minimal. Every day we would leave early in the morning, separate from each other, and spend the whole day alone in the forest. We'd come back at dusk, sit around the campfire, make a quick dinner from freeze-dried food, and then go to bed so we could wake up the next morning and do it all over again. That was the routine.

The foliage was peaking in Baxter, and the leaves of the upland birches were a brilliant yellow. The maples glowed orange and red. In two weeks, the colors would dull to russet and brown. Autumn storms would strip the trees. But for a week or two the forest flamed with color.

Days were crisp and cool, the sun warm. At night, the temperature dropped down into the twenties. I slept in a big square sleeping bag, draping a forty-below mummy bag over me when I started to feel chilled. I wore a hat, and I'd throw a parka over my head if it got really cold. I slept deeply, encased in a chrysalis of flannel and down.

It was an exciting time of year to observe moose. The rut made them particularly vocal and social. The cows lifted their big heads and bellowed, long echoing calls that came from deep in their chest cavities. The bulls made explosive grunting sounds in their throats that carried for miles.

I decide that I will get up before dawn and hike two miles up Mount Katahdin to photograph Basin Pond in the first light. The pond has excellent views of Katahdin's north-facing slopes.

Getting out of my sleeping bag into the cold predawn darkness is like jumping naked into a pool of icy water. The first thing that I put on that morning is my headlamp. It looks like a miner's lamp, cumbersome and heavy, with a round bulb set in a gaudy yellow rectangular casing. It straps around my head on a 1.5-inch-wide black and yellow elastic band and holds four AA batteries. It throws a good, strong light. Headlamps free up both hands. I don't want to be fumbling around with a flashlight, trying to get my gear together.

My pack is set. I carry a heavy 600 mm F4.5 lens, two 35 mm camera bodies, a 200 mm lens, a 100 mm lens, several wide-angle lenses, and a big Gitzo tripod. My pack must weigh forty pounds. I make cheese sandwiches and bring some cookies for lunch, and, of course, a couple of chocolate bars. I eat a lot of chocolate when I'm working. It keeps me going.

I lace my boots, heft my pack, and wonder for the hundredth time if it really needs to be so heavy. I hear Bill turn in his sleeping bag and grumble as the light from my headlamp flashes across his face. I start up Chimney Pond Trail, into the last hours of the night, no false dawn showing yet in the starlit sky. My icy breath steams in the headlamp's bright cone of light. My ankles and knees slowly adjust to the hard-packed earth of the trail that runs steeply upward.

I periodically flick off the headlamp, letting my body gather the sensory data it needs to move unerringly up the starlit trail, which climbs nearly a thousand feet in its first mile. Katahdin is a lone mountain; no big peaks surround it. It rises to 5,267 feet, a massive presence with thin ridges running parallel to its summit. Its wide shoulders roll down to high valleys thick with hardwoods. The mountain is an island unto itself, floating in the middle of the great north woods, a relatively pristine environment. In a state that has been mercilessly logged, Katahdin is an oasis, a world within a world.

I strip down as I climb, strapping my parka and underjacket to my pack, keeping a steady pace without taking rests or breaking a sweat. I don't want to get wet and chilled. But I do want to catch the first light for my photos, and, as usual, I haven't given myself quite enough time.

The sky is starting to turn light. I flick off my headlamp. My breathing is deep and long, my heart working hard to sustain the pace. The trail is worn from thousands of previous boot steps. It winds and turns, skirting Roaring Brook for the first mile, then breaking away to cut upward through steep, rocky terrain. The forest is mostly maple and birch with some mountain ash and viburnums.

Most of the trees are young and small. It's a harsh climate here. High winds continually try to beat the forest into submission. The young trees crowd together as if holding on to each other, branch to branch, root to root, in defiance of wind, ice, and snow.

Stars fade. The light comes fast now, always inexorable, always miraculous. I'm not sure I'm going to make it to where I want to be. I may miss what photographers think of as the magic hour.

The magic hour occurs just before the sun moves over the horizon. This is one of the prime times for landscape photography. Before you can see the sun, while it is still below the horizon, light starts to bathe the mountain with an effervescent, almost excruciating beauty. With the fall foliage peaking, the magic hour should be particularly dramatic. I walk faster and faster, pushing myself, ignoring the fact that I'm starting to sweat.

I come to the pond. It's about a quarter-mile long, a high-elevation, crystal-clear mountain pond, bordered by boulders, surrounded by stunted forest. Deadwood hugs the shores, beaten down by the harsh climate and bleached a silver-white from the action of sun, water, and wind. The air is still, the pond is calm. It looks very cold and very deep. I've just made it. It's starting to get light. I hurry to set up.

The light brightens on the eastern horizon. All but the brightest stars have fled. The sky is indeterminate, a blue-gray that is almost colorless, a suspension of color. I had hoped there would be some mist on the pond, but it's a very clear dawn: no clouds in the sky, nothing but the sun reflecting off the water. I'm set, waiting for the magic, but it doesn't happen. The light is flat. There's no glow or depth.

Nonetheless, it's a beautiful morning. The air moves, tumbling over itself, then gusting with small puffs, moving and freshening as the world tilts on its axis and the sun edges up, cresting the low ridges to the south, streaming across the yellows, reds, and golds of the Great North Woods. I sit on a rock at the pond's edge, the sun slanting over my right shoulder, drinking in the beauty of the morning.

A hawk slides through the air above the wide valley, almost flush against the mountain's polished face. The light now is sharp and crisp. I eat a piece of chocolate. The hawk dives.

I continue up the mountain, to a spot I know where the moose feed on willows and birches. It's a secret area, off trail. It's still early. Paulette must be curled up in bed at home with the extra blankets she uses when I'm not there. I can see her naked and inviting. I catch myself lost in thought and imagery. I stop in my tracks and bring myself back to the present moment. I carefully sniff the air. Scent it. Smell it. I take several short inhalations through the nose to complete one breath, bringing my attention to my breath, my breath bringing me back into the moment.

My hike continues. The trail levels, and I slow, looking for moose. I'm in a very young part of the forest. The area may have been blown down by storms or burned: Baxter has not been cut for many decades. This area has a lot of deadwood, trees from one to six inches in diameter lying across each other in what looks like an impenetrable maze. Dead snags, still standing, are interspersed with live birches. I find myself on a high spot in the trail looking down at this terrain.

Four or five hundred feet into this thick scrub I see a moose. It never ceases to amaze me how moose, big as they are, seem to be able to move through forest so thick that I wouldn't even want to think about traversing it. This moose seems to be ambling along, biding his time.

I follow him with a pair of compact seven-power binoculars. The moose looks tall and lean. I can just make out undeveloped antlers on its head. It must be a young bull, entering its second winter.

I watch him through the binoculars for a couple of minutes, and then he lays down. Deadwood and birches block my view. I wonder if I can get near to photograph him in his lay. I start into the tangle, but it's too thick. So I head back into the forest, approaching the bull in a roundabout way. I follow a dried-up streambed, a wash littered with stones. The going is much easier here.

I break out of the treeline, at the edge of the blowdown, and scan the terrain for the moose. There he is! He hasn't moved. I go slowly toward him, moving at an angle, as though I'm looking for something in the brush. I keep my attention off him, at a tangent. I tack like a sailboat, stopping often, until I'm within forty feet of him. I don't want to get too close too fast. I was charged by a large bull moose once, and Bill Fournier was chased up a tree by a moose cow. Moose can be unpredictable. Sometimes cows and younger bulls are more dangerous and unpredictable than large bulls. The young bulls can become irritated. They may be having a hard time dealing with the big bulls that monopolize the cows, dominating the rut. The young bulls have all their hormones going, but no release!

I watch carefully for warning signs of aggression in this young bull. Before attacking, moose usually flatten their ears. Hair bristles on their back. They show the whites of their eyes. This young bull, however, makes none of these signs. He simply observes me as I set up my equipment and photograph him. He is so unconcerned with my presence that he falls asleep, tucking his head next to his belly. His antlers are tiny and stunted. They looked deformed, perhaps four inches tall. It's about noon. I decide to lunch next to the moose, and he continues sleeping as I eat. It's very companionable, dining *al fresco* with a sleeping moose.

It's time to move on. I assemble my gear, without abrupt movements or noise. The moose sleeps on. Continuing down the dried streambed, I find wallows, also called rut pits, where bulls during the fall mating season have scraped the ground with their front hooves and urinated. The wallows in which the bulls and cows will roll are the size and shape of shallow bathtubs. In other areas, there are scrapes, places where bulls have scraped the ground and urinated, but where there is no rolling.

Wallows play an interesting part in moose courtship. In the area I'm traversing, Bill Byrne had come across a cow and a bull. The cow was browsing on birch and mountain ash. The bull started making a pit, digging at the dirt with his front hooves. The cow softly mooed, but made no move toward the bull. The bull made a second pit, several feet away from the first. He squatted over the pit and urinated into it. The cow mooed again and then rushed to the bull's side, circling him and mooing softly. She nudged the bull out of the pit and, as he stood by, dropped down into it, wallowing with her head and neck, rubbing against the fresh urine and dirt, mooing and grunting. She then lay down in the pit. The bull moved a short distance away and lay down facing her. About ten minutes later, the cow got up, went over to the bull, and rubbed her muzzle on his antlers. They touched muzzles, and she returned to the pit.

The poplar, willow, and birch in this area are favorite foods of the moose, and the trees are heavily browsed. Incisor scrapes are feathered, shoulder high, in the bark of young aspen. The woods open into an area of low shrubs and leatherleaf, which is between knee and waist high. It's slow going with my heavy pack, pushing through the tangle. At times I walk on top of the vegetation, balancing on the springy tufts of small bushes. There are traps in the thickets, sinks that my legs slip into that feel like manacles on my ankles. I yank free from them, trying not to crash forward into brush. My shins suffer a few scrapes, but nothing serious.

In spots, the shrubbery is lower and I'm able to move more quickly. The area was disturbed at one time, probably by a landslide. Boulders are jumbled across the scrubby plain. They seem to have come down off the mountainside. Katahdin is like that. Though not particularly high compared to other mountains around the world and relatively easy to climb, Katahdin has qualities of a much bigger mountain—rock slides, raging storms, and avalanches.

Across this open area, to the south, is a view of Katahdin's summit and north-facing slopes. There's a dusting of snow on the mountain's flanks, rivulets of white etched into the crannies and grooves of the mountainside. I start to photograph the shimmering swaths of yellow birches and the delicate white veins of snow, when I see the same young bull moose I had encountered earlier coming out of the forest, almost on the same path that I had taken—and he's coming straight toward me.

I think that he's going to veer off, since I'm in clear view, doing nothing to disguise my presence. But he walks slowly toward me, with a loose-limbed swaying gait that manages to be both majestic and ungainly. His anvil of a head is held high. His thick hooves make small explosions in the underbrush. His breath comes in huffs from the fist of his muzzle.

He stops twenty feet from me and turns sideways. This bull is still young, but big. His gangly legs look like they can barely support the huge barrel of his body. There's a hump on his back, almost like a half-formed camel's hump. His shoulders are higher than my head. His antler tips are seven feet off the ground. I would guess he weighs close to seven hundred and fifty pounds.

I photograph him—the picture you see at the beginning of this chapter—and he turns toward me again. What is this moose doing? I'm starting to worry. There are no trees to climb. No place to run. I could jump up and down and scream and yell, but I'm not sure what effect that would have. Is he threatening me? I'm not sure.

My heartbeat accelerates. I feel light, with energy flowing through me. My focus narrows. The world becomes very small. There is no room for thought. Everything seems suspended, with no sense of time passing.

I look up into the moose's eyes. They are deep and soft. They don't contain a shred of malice or negative intent. They are a mystery. I would give anything for a message. If his ears had turned back on his head it would have said *run!* But there's nothing. The moose is a cipher. He comes closer until the only thing between us is my tripod. He stops three feet from me. We stare at each other. I'm intimidated. He could do anything. I start backing away slowly. I don't want to make any sudden movements, and I also don't want to leave my expensive camera, mounted on the Gitzo, right under his nose. I grab one of the tripod's legs. As I pick it up, moving away from the moose, the tripod's other leg rocks off the ground, swinging toward him.

He rears up, all seven hundred and fifty pounds of him, kicking out with his hooves. I run backwards. So does he. We each run about twenty feet and stop, taking it all in. Now there's about forty feet between us. I've got my camera, but my open backpack is still out there, with all my camera gear. The moose faces me. I expect him to leave, but he walks over to my pack, bends his enormous snout toward my thousands of dollars of camera gear, and starts sniffing it.

I don't like this at all.

"Hey, moose! Hey! Get away from there!" I cry.

He raises his head and looks at me, very directly. And then, as I stand there in wonder, he lumbers over until he's standing directly in front of me again! He's three feet away and we're gazing into each other's eyes. Now what? I don't want to repeat the previous scenario. For reasons that I still can't fathom, I don't want the bull to make the first move. Maybe I need to take the initiative. So I put my hand out, very, very slowly. The moose inclines his nose. The world compresses as we get closer and closer, and then my hand touches the soft fuzz of his muzzle.

A jolt of energy surges in both of us! I see it burst in him. He jumps, twirling like a bucking bronco, kicking his heels in the air, spinning wildly. I jump back, running and breathless, exploding with that same energy.

In that moment, we share what I like to think of as a similar exhilaration. It looks like the moose is saying, "Yahoo! Yahoo! I did it!" And I feel that, too. I've watched cows when a bull is next to them and exciting them and their juices are flowing. This is exactly what I've seen them do: twirl and kick, twirl and kick.

Across species lines the moose and I connected in some fundamental way, perhaps even a life-altering way. What drew us toward each other, across a gulf of apprehension and distrust? What lifted my hand up toward his nose, and what inclined his nose toward me? And what most of the time keeps us from experiencing this same exhilarating connection with the natural world and with each other? This connection is life itself, and when it's sundered or absent we are only half alive. What keeps us in this moribund state so much of the time?

The moose leaves, ambling back into the Katahdin forest, and I look for a comfortable place among the rocks and meadowsweet to sit, a spot where I can keep my back straight and be comfortable for about thirty minutes. I need to let my body relax and my mind slow. I find such a spot and detach from the thoughts arising in my mind. I meditate on what keeps us from connecting with others and with the world around us. I realize the question has already been answered! *Attachment* flashes in the mirror of the mind: *attachment,* which says I am me and separate from you, whether the you is the bull moose or another human being. I am suddenly aware of the deep connection I share with all living things. With this awareness, I am flooded with compassion, a compassion that transcends pity.

Pity involves feeling sorry for something or someone. It is an emotion that contains within it a kind of condescension. "I'm up here and you're down there," pity seems to say. "Poor you!" Self-pity does the same thing. It says, "Poor me!" Pity separates the person who has pity from the person who receives it.

Compassion, on the other hand, is an understanding of the unity of all things. It is an awareness that *I* is not separate from *thou,* that whatever is happening to the planet, or to another person, is happening to me. Compassion is total empathy, an absolute sense of connection.

Let me compare pity and compassion through the following example. One summer morning, I stepped outside and heard an unworldly, totally unfamiliar crying sound, not very loud, but strange enough to stop me in my tracks. I looked in the direction of the sound but saw nothing except an open area of grass and pine needles. I didn't dare move. Again, I heard a distressed crying, a sound neither human nor animal. I saw nothing until I noticed the grass move, which I attributed to the wind. I waited until I heard the cry again, then slowly turned my body in its direction. I was amazed to see a toad being swallowed by a garter snake!

The snake's jaw had dislocated to accommodate the size of the toad; it had already swallowed the toad's left hind foot and one third of its body. The toad alternated between helplessly struggling to extricate itself from the snake's jaws and bleating its mournful cry while lying still. It seemed to be pleading for me to do something. I felt overwhelmed with pity for this toad, crying for its life.

To rescue it was my first inclination, and I came very close to intervening in the drama of the snake and the toad. But there was a larger picture here. Before my very eyes the toad was becoming the snake. The toad had hunted, killed, and eaten many insects, which had become the living toad. The snake, by eating the toad, became the toad and the insects, and the snake, in turn, would be fair game for a hawk or owl.

I was witness to an ancient and sacred ritual, something that could not and must not be stopped. Recognizing and accepting the interconnection of these lives allowed me to have as much compassion for the snake as I did for the toad.

We can carry this sense of interconnection into the human realm. One of my favorite poems is by Thich Nhat Hanh, called "Please Call Me By My True Names." In the poem, Thich Nhat Hanh speaks of being both prey and predator, both a twelve-year-old refugee and the sea pirate who rapes her. As I see it, the poem describes an understanding of the interconnection of all life and demonstrates that true compassion is not circumstantial or okay to have for one person but not another. This is very hard for most of us to accept until we understand our true nature. When we realize that we are not separate from one living thing, that we *are* both the pirate and the girl, only then are we able to have true compassion.

I don't want to gloss over the complex differences here between the snake I saw and the pirate. The snake is programmed to survive, fulfilling its animal needs. As such, it's easier to have compassion for the snake than for the pirate, who seems to be choosing to be cruel, to exercise his power in ways that are unnecessarily hurtful. In raping the girl, the pirate forsakes the unity, the sense of connection exemplified when the moose and I touched. The pirate is disconnected, an isolated little island, which is what most of us are.

In the pirate's case, this isolation and disconnection are extreme. His brutality and power continually demonstrate to others that he is a force to be reckoned with. The pirate's mind-set is "I am mean and merciless. If you're not with me, you're against me. If you're against me, I will destroy you." It's the way the pirate gains respect and security in his world, a world that is about power and domination.

To appear weak in the pirate's world—a world of predators—means not being able to survive. It means being preyed upon. To survive among predators, you must be a predator, preying upon the weak. The pirate doesn't know sensitivity, love, or compassion, which have no value in his world. If you grew up in the pirate's compassionless world, you too would likely become a pirate.

The pirate is an absolutely terrified human being. He is not just running from fear, he is in an all-out stampede from it. He is afraid for his own survival, afraid that if he's not brutal, he will be brutalized. In his poem, Thich Nhat Hanh recognizes this when he writes that the pirate's heart is "not yet capable of seeing and loving."

The pirate's lack of compassion has deep personal resonance for me. I have my own pirate and girl story, and it marked a dramatic turning point in my life.

My gang, the Devil's Disciples, had organized a big party with the Hell's Angels, to which all the most notorious motorcycle gangs on the East Coast were invited. It was a wild affair on a deserted part of a Cape Cod beach. It started on a Friday and went through Monday morning.

There was a tradition at these parties of taking a gallon bottle of wine and spiking it with whatever drugs people had on them: acid, speed, uppers, downers, anything that would dissolve. The wine bottle was passed around. Everyone would drink, and if you were smart you'd try, surreptitiously, not to drink too much. And you tried not to drink last, because the last drinker imbibed all the sediment on the bottle's bottom. At this party, my vice president drank last, and, I kid you not, it changed him. He wasn't right for years.

At the party, there were two Mamas (female groupies) from the Queens motorcycle club, one older and one younger. Strange as it sounds, the gang had many unwritten, but understood, codes of behavior. One of the codes of behavior in the world of the bike clubs for a Mama (who, it is important to remember, has chosen to be a Mama) was sex on demand with any and all gang members. Within the perimeters of our world, this code made sense. The Mama wasn't allowed to prefer one "brother" to another. That would have meant jealousies and territorial disputes. The fraternal order of the gang was unassailable.

Inside the fraternal order of the gang there was a real sense of compassion, but outside it there was almost no compassion. The compassion of the gangs is an extreme instance of compassion that is conditional, circumstantial, or bound to a particular situation. But it's important to recognize that a gang is a microcosm of feelings of nationalism, racism, or religious fanaticism, all of which create a lack of sensitivity and compassion.

At the party on Cape Cod, at some point during the evening, the younger of the two Queens Mamas grew tired of the constant demands of gang members. It was then that I made one of the biggest mistakes of my life. I asked the older Mama, who was supposed to be training the younger woman, "What are you going to do about that?"

The words came easy. But I didn't understand the implications of what I'd said. My question set in motion an appalling sequence of events, for which I blame myself.

"I'm going to take care of it," the older Mama told me.

Later that night, the older Mama stripped the younger Mama naked and started beating her. Some of the gang members joined in. The situation rapidly got out of hand. Some gang members needed to demonstrate their power and dominance, and when they saw weakness and vulnerability, they seized on it. The young Mama had transgressed their code—she was now on the outside. She was no longer worthy of their compassion. The scene became symbolic of the ways in which we all separate ourselves from the rest of humanity and from the rest of life, making judgments about people, saying this person is good and this person is bad, this person is beautiful and this person is ugly—all the circumstantial, superficial ways in which the thought process treats other people like objects and keeps us from having compassion for one person and not another, for the girl but not the pirate, the toad but not the snake.

The gang members taunted the young Mama with burning branches, and shot at her with handguns loaded with blanks. They made up a rule on the spot: if somebody "bought" the young Mama, she would belong to a brother, and they wouldn't harm a brother's "property." Bought, she would be back on the inside, back in the fold. There was a big fire and we were all gathered in a ring around it. The young Mama staggered, naked, from one person to the next, offering herself for sale.

"How much?" each brother asked.

"Five cents," she'd reply. But no one wanted to buy her. No one wanted to appear weak or soft. She made her pathetic offering, crying like the toad as it was being swallowed by the snake. She was coming to me, and, boy! I wanted to buy her. But my wife was sitting right next to me. The fact that I was married was a good rationalization for not buying the woman. And as president of my club, showing compassion in this situation would have branded me weak. It would have meant an unacceptable loss of face. I watched her coming toward me, and I could see in the eyes of some of the other brothers that they, too, were uncomfortable with what was happening. They had compassion for the young Mama. But, like me, they couldn't appear weak. They were too afraid.

The young Mama came to me. She was crying, cowering, her body scratched, bruised, and full of tremors.

"Will you buy me?" she asked.

I shook my head, and she staggered away to the next person.

Luckily, she eventually came to one of my gang members whose name was Stubby. The girls didn't like Stub. He was short and thick like a stump. He really wanted her, and he didn't care what anybody thought. He forked up the five cents, and she was his. They disappeared together into the night.

The next morning, the elder Mama made the young Mama clean the beach of the pond around which we were encamped. I was relieved to see that, aside from cuts, bruises, and an injured arm, the young Mama appeared to be okay, at least physically. What kind of damage she sustained to her spirit and psyche I'll never know.

As that young woman walked toward me in the firelight, I swore to myself that I would live out the compassion that I felt for the girl. The way I put it to myself at the time was that I was going to stand up for the truth, for what I believed was right, even if that meant that the image I had of myself would be damaged and I would be perceived as weak or soft. At the next meeting of area gang leaders, I told them that I didn't think what happened to the young Mama was cool. I didn't know it at the time, but what I was doing was one of the most courageous acts of my life. It was compassion itself that was courageous, not me. The power of compassion acted, not my sense of self. I could have been thrown out of the gang or beaten up, but, surprisingly, many of the leaders agreed that what had happened to the young Mama was unnecessary.

I know all too well that the gang members, myself included, were like Thich Nhat Hanh's pirate, acting from primarily psychological needs. The snake's needs, on the other hand, were physical: eat or die. It is imperative that if we are truly connected, if we have compassion, we let the snake swallow the toad, while we try to dissuade, distract, or stop the pirate or the gang. This understanding began to express itself in me the night I saw the young Mama brutalized.

Most of us will do whatever it takes to belong, to be accepted and respected. We will do whatever it takes for our image of ourselves to survive. It's a lot easier to do this when what is required of us is considered to be the norm, when "doing what it takes" is accepted and rewarded by our peers. Just think of what it would take for a pirate to stand up to the other pirates and say, "Hey, you guys, I don't think you should be hurting that little girl." Or for the gang leader to buy the young Mama. Or a businessman to put his job on the line to say, "I don't think we should be manufacturing cigarettes, they're killing a lot of people." It takes a lot of courage.

I know from my life, from my experience in the tough, brutal world of the gangs, that it is fear that stands in the way of compassion. Where there is fear, there is no compassion. The fear that I'm talking about here is the fear that results from the attachment we have to our need for others to accept our image. Can I let go of my image, my job, my status, power, money in the name of compassion or what I really think is right?

If we look deeply within ourselves, we will find the same process of adherence to image that we see in the pirate. When we are able to understand our own nature, how fragmented, isolated, and frightened we are, how alone and always striving for acceptance we are, then, and only then, can we begin to understand that the pirate's fear, the girl's fear, and the gang's fear are identical. Only then can we have true compassion.

We all have a responsibility to put an end to this fear in ourselves. When I put an end to it in me, I help the pirate and the girl, the gang and the Mama.

We are all connected in ways we don't always understand. Compassion is the awareness that, while there is one pirate left in the world raping one girl, we are all rapists and we are all being raped. We put an end to this vicious circle by understanding the pirate, understanding ourselves, and helping the pirate to understand himself.

Still sitting in the field, the moose long gone, my attention shifts toward the aspen leaves fluttering in the breeze. Light reflects from them and from the mountainside, glistening in thin wispy threads of snow that run down the grooves and cracks of Katahdin's massive north face. When the moose and I reached toward each other, when we touched, we both wanted to make contact. There was some kind of wonder and curiosity in both of us. We were both saying, What, *what* is this being? We were both in the same space—a kind of awe that was a suspension of thought and judgment. A state of pure inquiry.

It is in this state of pure inquiry that we connect. It is in this state that we see ourselves as both the pirate and the girl, the Mama crawling on her hands and knees and the Devil's Disciple gang leader, cowering with fear inside the tough image he projects, struggling with whether to stand up, to speak out, to be true to what he knows is right. It is in this state that we have compassion. It is in this state that the door of our heart swings open.

7.

―――

SPEAKING
WITHOUT WORDS

ACCORDING TO MOST DICTIONARIES, *COMMUNICATION* means an interchange of thoughts and opinions through shared symbols. But I want to go beyond this definition, beyond shared symbols, to *direct* communication. As I learned one winter from a red fox, thought is not always necessary for powerful, perhaps even life-altering, understanding.

The following story takes place in the winter of 1982. Back in those days, I spent lots of time learning the language of animal tracks, and following them wherever they took me. I was separated from my second family, living alone, driving a truck for a living, one week on, one week off. Money was tight, really tight. So much so, in fact, that it was difficult to find enough cash to put gas in my Jeep to go anywhere. So I found myself spending lots of time just hanging out with the wild animals, exploring the forest, and tracking.

One morning in early December I woke to find that it had snowed during the night. I dressed and walked outside, standing on a bluff over the Millers River, watching the storm clouds clear. The sun broke through widening fractures in the cloud cover. Dark shapes moved across the sky. Snow and the ripples on the river sparkled together: pinpoints of silver light exploding.

The snow had the kind of wet consistency that squeezes right down and holds a perfect track. You can see every little nuance of foot pattern and gait in this kind of snow. It's a tracker's dream. But like all dreams, it's ephemeral. To hold the animal tracks, the snow must stay wet and not melt, which means the temperature must hover just above freezing.

As I watched the storm clear, I knew that I would have to wait a day to begin tracking. The first day after a storm most animals would be holed up and they wouldn't begin to move until that night. With keen anticipation I followed the temperature. It held in the mid-thirties all day and into the evening. Before I went to sleep I checked it: thirty-seven degrees. The next morning, I could hardly believe the temperature had miraculously held above freezing. This was going to be one of those rare days that occurs maybe a few times each winter, if at all. Tracking conditions were perfect.

I packed up my gear and stepped outside, taking in the view. The river ran like a black ribbon through two glistening white flanks of ice. The ice shelves were jagged and erratic, sometimes cutting into the banks, sometimes thrusting out into the current that pushed against them. The river moved with a cold rushing sound.

I detected movement upriver to my left. A small black line moved along the ice shelf. A mink! It darted in and out of the water, never stopping for a second, looking here, looking there, diving into little crevices, dipping into the water, under the ice. The ice had pockets in it, caves that the mink seemed to be investigating. It moved quite close to me, maybe fifteen feet away. It didn't seem to know I was there, and then it was gone.

I start off through wet snow. I have no idea what I am going to track today. I'll take whatever nature offers. This not knowing is a wonderful feeling. Too often our lives are goal-oriented and structured, full of striving and wanting and needing things. Goals provide us a sense of security. If we have a blueprint of what we have to do for the day, it gives us a pattern to follow. We create patterns because they're familiar and safe. But living old patterns can take us out of the present and dull our awareness, the quality of attention that keeps us alive from moment to moment. It's a wonderful feeling, for me at least, to break patterns and feel the freedom that ensues.

I have an exercise on this theme that you might like to try. It's called Free Walking Meditation. It's about letting the forest speak to you without words, letting your own inner awareness direct you without conscious thought. Unlike some of my other meditations, which can be done in your backyard or in the confines of a city park, Free Walking Meditation requires a large swath of quiet woods, a map, and a compass. This meditation should be done alone, in silence.

The object of this exercise is to wander without any particular destination in mind. When you enter the woods, make sure to take a compass reading and check your point of entry on your map so you don't get lost. When you've finished, you need to be able to reenter the world.

Walk into the woods, away from the road. Leave the man-made world behind. Get away from the sounds of machines and human voices. Let the direction you're moving in happen by itself. Scent the air, sniffing it like an animal. This will increase your awareness and heighten your senses. Don't try to identify what you smell. Too often our tendency toward labeling shuts us off from the freshness of our sensations and the vitality of experience.

Be careful not to turn Free Walking into an activity with the purpose of achieving an awakening or some other kind of spiritual experience. It's not an aerobic workout, either. Drop those goals. As you walk deeper into the woods, monitor your thought process. That doesn't mean getting lost in thought and losing awareness of your surroundings. It does mean being present in the moment and spontaneous in your movement.

There is no destination in Free Walking Meditation, only exploration of your inner landscape. You are walking freely in the woods, not trying to go anywhere or do anything. You're just moving and breathing and smelling and hearing and letting the woods call to you. Perhaps you see a slight trail or a contour in the land that beckons. Follow it. You see a softness in the forest floor. Take off your shoes and walk on it. Sit down and close your eyes. Try moving very slowly, taking your time. But if you feel like running, run! Do whatever the forest urges you to do.

To finish the Free Walking Meditation, check your map and compass and make your way back to the point where you first entered the woods. You can do this meditation for several hours, or even a whole day.

I approach my day of tracking like an extended Free Walking Meditation. No pattern. No blueprint. No authority. No goal. The forest is calling. I move along the river, walking upstream, picking my way through hemlock forest. The path I'm walking along is obscure, a trail for wandering fishermen and hunters. I move slowly, ducking under overhanging branches, straddling deadfalls. The river flies by, turning and hissing. From a distance, I spot a line of tracks weaving through the woods. They appear as a delicate line of dots, each perfectly in front of the other. But as I close in on them I see that they are ever so slightly off kilter. Even in the distance, looking at the trail, I say *red fox*, the knowledge like a small explosion in my body.

There is a possibility that the tracks could be coyote. I've been fooled before. But on closer inspection I know, without a doubt, that the tracks were left by a red fox. The front heel is inscribed with a chevron, a boomerang shape. If there's one thing that says red fox, it's that little bar that shows up in the front heel pad.

I've found my trail for the day, but I have no idea where the fox's tracks will lead. This animal leaves a direct-registering trail—each track is really two tracks. As the fox walks or trots along, its front foot comes down and makes a track; its hind foot steps directly into that track. This is why the red fox is sometimes called a perfect walker. When the fox is in this gait it's normally trotting, moving quite a bit faster than you or I walk.

The trail appears fresh. I kneel next to the small mounds of kicked-up snow in front of the tracks, and I blow on the mounds. They hold their shape, which tells me the prints are over an hour old. Under most conditions it takes an hour or so for snow particles to adhere to each other and make the mound solid. I look at the fine edges and detail of the tracks. I can't see much sign of melting, and I surmise from this evidence that the tracks are probably less than eight hours old.

If I'd concluded that the trail was less than an hour old, I would have chosen to backtrack the fox, that is, track it in the opposite direction of where it was going. This is to avoid unnecessarily disturbing the animal. If you want to learn about the fox and how it lives its life, you don't want to interfere with its natural behavior. I've tracked an animal when it's aware of my presence, and all I've learned is how the animal is reacting to me!

I follow the fox trail away from the river into a forest of maple, oak, black birch, and ash. The ground is hilly, strewn with gray rocks. The fox picks up a deer run, stopping to urinate on a lone hemlock seedling that stands out from the other vegetation. The yellow specks of its urine do not project very far from its hind tracks. From this I deduce that the fox is a female. A male fox's urine would project for a greater distance. I bend down to smell the urine. It's what I expect— a pungent skunky smell unique to red fox.

The fox has proclaimed herself in many ways: through her trail, her movement, her urine's scent. She is telling me about her life. Her trail reveals her, communicating without words. I track on. She wheels and bounds back seven feet. There are four sets of prints in a close group. One front foot is forward of the other. The back feet register to either side and ahead of the front feet. To visualize this, think of the fox moving in a leap-frog position, front feet pushing off before her back feet even hit the ground.

The fox had heard something under the snow, most likely a vole, and had pounced. I check the snow for little vole tunnels, and there they are! I follow the fox downslope into a hollow where she breaks her gait again. She has broken her gait just twice, once to urinate and once to pounce. Now, suddenly, her tracks widen. I know that she's abruptly slowed. Her trail says: *caution*. Then I see why. We're at the beginning of a pool. The fox has sensed thin ice under the snow cover. Her wide gait spread her weight.

She may hazard the ice, but not I! Cautiously, I move around the pool's edge, thick with arrowwood. I pick up the fox's trail at the pool's end, and I track her up a steep embankment to a railroad bed.

She inspects a ruffed grouse roost under a leaning oak tree. Luckily for the grouse, it had left the roost before the fox appeared. I don't often find evidence of fox killing grouse, but occasionally the fox gets lucky. I've seen grouse feathers in fox scat.

The fox trots off, her prints a clean narrow line in the snow. I've followed her for several hours. I feel close to her, as though I've made a friend, become intimate with someone. I've walked many miles with the fox. Reading her track and sign, I've felt in my body her excitement and wild bounding in pursuit of the vole, her curiosity at the grouse roost. Her tracks reveal her life to me. The experience of tracking her is a book with its own language, an experiential account of direct communication that I embrace with my whole being. Tracking has made me intimate with the fox in a way that is more precise and personal than words.

I've traveled deep into the woods. I break for lunch, eating slowly. The sun warms my cheeks, and I doze, wind sighing in the treetops. When I wake I'm so comfortable that I almost expect to find myself in my bedroom. I feel grateful that I am so at home in this wild place.

I deeply inhale the cool clean air. The day is trickling, vibrating. The snow is porous. It breathes as the sun warms it. A balmy breeze blows from the west. The sky is clear, the air dry, but moisture rises from the ground as the snow melts. I can taste the moisture in my mouth. A single leaf dangles from the limb of a lone beech, its bark silvery, smooth, and gleaming with trickling water rolling down its bark from its sunny crown.

I follow the fox upland through a forest of maple and oak, until she lays up on a south-facing slope. The lay is a round depression in the snow, about twelve inches in diameter. In it, I find several long white hairs from the tip of the fox's tail embedded in the snow, an unintentional gift. I look down at the lay, transfixed. The fox has slept there in a tight little ball, her head curled into her body, her long bushy tail swept over her nose and ears, her wide eyes closed tight, breath shallow in sleep, auburn fur thick and bristling.

Leaving the lay, the fox skirts the top of a ledge. Some of the rock is bare. There may have been a fire here long ago. Her trail ends in a small cave that runs straight down into the rock. Unless there's a back entrance, I know she's still in there. I circle the area to see whether there's a back way out. I'll find tracks if she's left. There are none. I can't quite believe it. Seldom do you follow a trail directly to an animal.

I want to prove that she's there. As I shine my flashlight into the den's entrance, it dislodges an icicle, sending it skittering down into the dark twisting tunnel. From the depths of the den comes a little muffled bark.

There's no doubt about it—she's there! I feel a little guilty about my intrusion. But I'm so excited about the bark! It's a big climax to my day of tracking. I slowly hike back to the house on an old logging road. That evening, I find myself wondering whether I had actually heard that muffled bark. It was so short and quick. Was the fox really there? She must have been. But I still can't quite believe it.

The next morning the temperature has dropped below thirty-two degrees, but I'm still hoping for some good tracks to follow. Stepping outside I can see my breath. And I realize upon inhaling, wow, fox scent! It's heavy in the air. Its skunky odor drives all thoughts from my head.

The smell comes from a little knoll that overlooks my house. I walk up the hill and see fox tracks etched in the snow. A fox has paced back and forth in full view of my house, urinating over and over. All I smell is fox and suddenly, I know this fox. An overwhelming knowledge of fox rushes into me. There is nothing intellectual about this knowledge—it is preverbal, no syntax needed. *Fox! Fox! Fox!* cries the scent that saturates the cold morning air. I breathe it into my body.

It is, I realize, the fox from the day before. She is telling me that the forest that we both inhabit is as much hers as it is mine. This lesson is driven into me in a way that is deeper than words. The fox has taught me in its own way—direct, undeniable, with no room for error. There was no exchange of thoughts or opinions. There was no reasoning. The mechanism that tries to find reasons for everything had come to a stop. The fox and I communicated from the mutual awareness that all beings share. I would say *real* communication is this awareness—a consciousness that *is* our connection with all living things.

The fox had traveled a lot that night. When I returned to her den site, I saw more than one trail leading to and coming from the cave. I knew that I wouldn't be able to track her as neatly and cleanly as I had the day before, and I felt I should give her some space. So that day I went off in search of other tracks.

It's amazing how much wordless conversation exists without our being conscious of it. We are constantly communicating to each other through facial expressions, eye movements, body language, and our energy level. Often, our silence can say much more than our sentences.

As individuals can communicate without words, so, too, can a group of people. Speaking with and without words was paramount to maintaining my onetime status in the 1960s as leader of the two motorcycle gangs. As a gang leader, I had to have a good "feel" for the gang as a whole. In order to maintain control of a very rebellious lot, I had to be acutely aware of any effect I was having on them.

I had to know exactly what to say at all times and, perhaps even more important, how to carry myself. If, at some point, the group members doubted my ability to lead, I would have to demonstrate my leadership qualities. Exhibiting exceptional riding skills always worked well. I would wildly spin my bike in skids and turns, revving the throttle like Evel Kneivel. I'd stand up on my seat while leading the pack through the center of town.

Rosemary, my wife at the time, and I used to do stunts on my bike that established us the alpha pair in the gang. She'd sit up on my shoulders while I stood upright on the pegs of the bike, my arms extended out to either side. We'd ride down the highway like this. The other gang members couldn't do these stunts, and they lived vicariously through me and Rosemary, turning me into a hero and identifying with me, so that my stunts were their stunts. They shared in my ability and charisma. They called me "Capone" after the gangster Al Capone.

One of the most persuasive ways in which I'd establish my authority was to challenge all comers to a drag race. We raced at Horseneck Beach on an eighth-of-a-mile run. Over that short distance a bike, with its quick acceleration, has an advantage over a car. The track was a huge parking lot that the state had built, a great swath of asphalt behind dunes that led to a sandy beach.

The bikes we rode were incredibly powerful, responsive machines. The trick was knowing how to let the throttle go, full blast, right on the starting line, and bingo! pop the clutch. Most people couldn't do it. It took timing, guts, control, and practice.

My Harley was part of me. My self-image was intimately tied to that hunk of gleaming iron with its shining chrome and powerful roaring engine. The sound of the engine was a song of power, a song of machismo. That bike was the foundation of my image of myself, the source of my strength.

When we raced, we'd post lookouts on the top of the dunes who could spot any police cruiser coming in. We had the whole place to ourselves, and hundreds of people and cars would fill the lot. Racers came with the fastest cars and the fastest bikes. I'd go down there with my boys. There'd be about twelve or fifteen of us, riding in a line like we were the boss of the whole place. The cars would be dragging, revving their engines. They'd race through a tunnel of people, thick on either side. There were no fences and no boundaries. Had one of the cars lost control, got a flat tire, or just veered slightly, it would have mowed right into the crowd at high speed.

I vividly remember what it felt like to be there on the starting line with the guy next to me in a hot souped-up car revving his pipes while the crowd screamed. A girl would always start the race by lifting a flag up over her head. It wavered there, like the suspended blade of a guillotine. As she swept the flag downward, my cycle would be wide open, the clutch popping out and my weight not on the bike because the rear wheel needed to spin or I'd go head over heels into the asphalt with the Harley on top of me.

The car next to me would smoke rubber, but not for long because my bike would bolt forward, back tire burning, and I'd put my weight down and take off. I'd make sure the front wheel stayed on the ground at least some of the time. When I'd shift into second, the front wheel would come off the ground, into the air. It was like an airplane takeoff.

In race after race, I'd wipe out every car there. And if there were other bikes there I'd wipe them out, too. When the races were over, I'd be top dog. When my boys were satisfied that I had beaten everybody, they'd start chanting "Capone! Capone! Capone!" Then the crowd would start chanting "Capone! Capone! Capone!"

Think of the momentum—the leadership quality I expressed through winning those races. All that energy and all that imagery and all that power is what I used to control my gang and maintain my "alpha dog" status. The group members did what I told them to do. They listened when I spoke. They looked up to me. It was all created with language that was deeper than words.

After the race, I'd do my stunts, riding the bike down on its side, standing up on the seat, skidding (cutting donuts, we called it), doing wheelies. The crowd would go wild. At the end of all this my guys would fall in behind me and we'd ride out of there, a thundering convoy of iron, leather, long hair, and beards, feeling like we ruled the world.

These were the cards I'd play to communicate that I was the gang leader, to exert my authority and preeminence. This was a process of building an image, something that I held up for everyone to see.

Look at the image I was selling to my gang. It may have been appropriate in a wolf pack, and even at some level of human behavior, but for us to learn what it means to live in harmony with the natural world and each other, we have to go beyond selling images to each other and begin to understand direct communication. Images of ourselves rarely communicate who we really are. In my biker days I had an image of myself as a real cool biker and, even more than that, as the leader of the pack. All I cared about was my self-image. If someone supported my image, I liked him. If he didn't support it, I didn't like him. If someone hurt my feelings, I didn't want him to know it because it showed weakness on my part. Not only did I hide my hurt, but I couldn't even allow myself to feel the hurt, and I suppressed my real feelings.

The person who hurt my feelings didn't have a clue as to how I really felt because I hid behind my image. We all do this. At some point, when our suppressed emotions explode, no one understands the problem because the true situation is hidden under layers of self-concern.

Let's say we could sweep all these images that we are attached to, everything we identify with, into a little corner of the inner landscape. The images are not completely gone, but they're no longer in the driver's seat. We are aware of their presence, their influence, their bias. If we succeed in knocking these images out of control, then there is incredible sensitivity. There is an intimacy with all that we are. We are no longer living according to the perspective of these images, but from a place that is simply *aware* of the whole mess.

This is a radical change. When you hurt me, I realize and accept that I am hurt. There is no need to hide it from myself or from you. I'm in direct communication with what's going on in me—I'm living the wild within. If you are fully aware of who you are, there can be some direct communication between us. A relationship between us can proceed honestly.

Not only can self-images get in the way of connecting with others, but they are also a hindrance to connecting with nature. We can't wake up to who we really are if we are caught up in playing a role or sticking to an image. If we're attached to being a writer, a lawyer, a good person, a bad person, if we cling to some quality of self that is precious to us (if we're invested in being leader of the pack), then there is no room for communion with nature and with each other.

How can we get beyond self-images to direct communication? When we try to do this, we often fall into the trap of creating a new image to replace the old one. You may even create an image of yourself as being a person who is beyond images! You may devise an exercise to get rid of the images, while all the time you'll be creating new ones. If you see *this* (the fact that images are trying to get rid of images) then there is direct communication with these images. They are seen for what they are. Their limitations are exposed. They are swept into the corner. Each time you create a new image, it too can be swept into the corner by recognizing what it is.

When someone devises an exercise to get rid of his self-images, it is these images that are asking for the exercise. If I give that person an exercise, a practice, those images may end up being strengthened. But if we enlarge the images, they may get big enough so that they are easier to see and therefore easier to understand. The story below illustrates this point.

A wandering Buddhist monk finds himself at the gates of a lone monastery deep in the snowy mountains of northern Japan. He had never heard of the monastery and there was no name at the entrance. He stayed at the gate for days without food before someone let him in. Then he was led to the head monk who asked what he wanted. The wandering monk said, "Master, teach me silence. Teach me how to stop these images and this constant movement of thought so that I may know peace."

The master replied, "Young man, I will give you an exercise. Go to the corner of your room and sit. Make your back straight and watch your thoughts. Do not miss a single one of them. And most of all, do not interfere with them. Except there is one thought

you must not have. Do not think of gorillas. Go and do this med-
itation morning and night."

The wandering monk didn't ask any questions. He practiced
faithfully. But something was definitely wrong because he'd never
thought about gorillas before, and now his meditation was full of
them!

He went to the master. "Master, help me," he said. "I must be
doing something wrong in my meditation. I keep thinking about
gorillas, the one thought you said I must not have!"

The old master's eyes were deep, silent, and direct. He replied,
"Keep meditating."

The young man kept practicing. He was fighting hard for
peace, but all he kept thinking about were gorillas. He saw big go-
rillas and little gorillas, gorillas swinging on trees and beating
their chests, gorillas sitting zazen and meditating on gorillas! He
was even having nightmares about gorillas, and the word gorilla
was always on the tip of his tongue. He felt an irrepressible urge to
shout "Gorilla!" and shatter the silence of his room. He was in
more conflict than ever, and thought he might be losing his mind.
He went back to the master and reiterated his pleas. The master's
reply was the same as before: "Keep meditating!"

The young monk was becoming desperate. He saw gorillas
walking in the wooded grounds of the monastery, looking at him
with sad black eyes. Everyone knew that there were no gorillas in
the mountains of northern Japan.

The wandering monk went back to see the old master. There
were tears in his eyes. "Master," he said, "I've tried to stop the im-
ages of gorillas, but they keep appearing before me. Please tell me
what I'm doing wrong. Please help me!"

The old master had given the young monk a chance to see. All

the master could do was to emphasize the problem, put a magnify-
ing glass to it. The master was very clear about the fact that the
wandering monk had to see the truth for himself.

Almost shouting, the master spoke. "Won't you ever learn? You
cannot control your thoughts."

Images are ideas. They are created by the movement of thought. When we try to get rid of images, thought is trying to control thought, self is trying to control self—the wandering monk's dilemma. Although this looks like a futile, circular process, self was also getting worn down during the young monk's practice because self was in conflict. The more the monk tried to control the situation (that is, not think of gorillas while he meditated), the more obvious it became that he couldn't. As long as his spiritual pride was wrapped up in becoming a good meditator, this image wouldn't let him see his inability to control and quiet his mind.

In this light, I am going to give you an exercise called Image Tracking. This is not an exercise that is done for fun. It's serious and, in some sense, a matter of life and death, the life and death of who you think you are. You will want to do this exercise with one other person. Pick someone you think you know well, and with whom you have a healthy and loving relationship. The closer you are emotionally, the better. This exercise can be very powerful. It may open some sore points in your relationship, or it may deepen it in a profound way. What happens will depend on your commitment to communication.

Begin this exercise by making a list of the images you have of your partner—the characteristics you would use to describe him or her, i.e., smart, gullible, competent, domineering, etc. Write another list describing yourself, and a third list of the characteristics you think your partner has written describing you.

Each of you now has three lists of images. Exchange them with your partner and discuss them. Get ready for some possible surprises and, potentially, some strong emotions. You may have a very real opportunity to learn about your images, your attachments to your images, and just what is and is not being communicated about these images. Did your list of what you thought your partner thought of you match what he actually did think about you? How much of your relationship is invested in these images?

You can do this exercise once a month. In between sessions, try to change the images or get rid of them in order to get to a place with your partner where you connect directly, beyond your images, in a place where what you *think* about your partner doesn't interfere with the communication between you.

8.

THE DANCE OF
LIFE AND DEATH

DEATH IS SOMETHING A LOT OF PEOPLE PREFER NOT TO talk about. We even avoid the word itself. Instead of saying "my mother died," we'll say "she passed away" or "she is no longer with us" or "her body passed on but she's still with us in spirit."

We remove ourselves from death in ways we may not even realize. Consider the food that we eat to sustain ourselves. We take ourselves farther and farther away from the slaughterhouse. Most of us have never seen one, because the grocery store is such a convenient place to pick up all the dead things that keep us alive. We don't even have to kill all the dead things. Someone else's hands do it for us. Neatly packaged and wrapped, no blood on our hands, no soil to till, no compost to turn.

Psychologically, we avoid death too. We create all kinds of belief systems—in life after death or in reincarnation—to shield us from the inevitable. We fear death because it is unknown, and the unknown is where thought cannot go. Thought and the structure of our belief systems give a sense of bringing the unknown into the known, thereby making it somewhat safe and comfortable and familiar.

Life is impossible without death. Just as there is no back without a front, no number one without a zero, there is no life without death. Life and death are not separate, but a continuum. It doesn't make sense to embrace one and avoid the other. We must acknowledge both, or our lives will be fragmented and we will remain in fear. We must understand what death really is to be free of our fear of what we think death is.

Hunter-gatherer societies lived very close to the continuum of life and death. These people were a constant witness to the sacrifice of plants and animals at the altar of their own lives. With their hands they pulled and cut plants from the life-giving soil. Their arrows stopped the hearts of animals, and they would then remove the animals' entrails, their bodies still warm with life. The warmth of their own lives was ensured by the hides of the animals. They knew that they could not live unless the animals lived. They knew the animals lived because plants and other animals had died and become their flesh.

In modern society we are far removed from these primordial connections to the plants and animals. We eat, drive our cars, and build our houses, sometimes totally insensitive to the beings that have died to keep it all going, as though they are inexhaustible and of no consequence. There remains no sense of the sacred.

To understand the continuum of life and death, and the dance between the two, is to bring the sacred back into our lives. The following story and exercise are aimed at helping clarify and recast the way we think about life and death, giving us a clear sense of their inseparable relationship.

I wake before first light to track deer. It's a bitter February morning, and the bedroom is cold. I slip from the cocoon of heavy wool blankets, from the warm place next to Paulette. Shivering, I pad into the kitchen. The thermometer mounted on the frosted window reads four degrees above zero. I step outside for a moment, testing the cold air. Big white pines tower on the bluff, dark forms rising to the glitter of stars.

The two-foot snowpack is topped with fresh flakes from a recent flurry. The river hisses nearby, its current crackling in the cold. Ravens caw, a croaking, guttural sound that rasps, chatters, and ascends, complex vocalizations that evoke the wild to me just like the wolf's howl or the tremolo of loons.

I'm tracking deer for the Metropolitan District Commission, which wants to determine the winter food habits, habitat use, and behavior of the reservation's white-tailed deer population in response to the growing alarm among Quabbin foresters that deer are culling valuable hardwood saplings. It is 1987. My pay is $1,500 for two hundred and fifty hours of fieldwork.

At this point in our lives, Paulette and I live "off the grid," generating our own electricity with two generators in the cellar: a large on-demand Kohler four-cylinder flathead that runs on propane and a small Honda one-cylinder gas-powered model attached to twelve-volt rechargeable marine batteries.

As I wash my hands and face, the Kohler kicks in, powering the pump that sends water up into the house from our shallow filtration well. I set my meditation zafu (a firm round pillow) in the corner of our narrow living room, barely wide enough to contain a couch. I no longer sit cross-legged when I meditate because my knees are wrecked from doing hand-balancing, full lotus asanas during the ashram phase of my life.

Kneeling, I place the zafu between my knees and begin. I sit for thirty-five minutes, making no attempt to manipulate what's arising in my mind. I key into my thought process, what's happening inside me. I pay attention to what arises in my mind.

Thoughts arise and fall away. The death of these thoughts is as important as their being. I acknowledge the whole of life, follow the movement of life and death, bowing three times in gratitude to all the beings who have given up their lives to make my life possible.

The sky is a gray smudge upriver where ravens nest and the sun will rise. I eat a big breakfast, loading up on bran muffins warmed in the oven, which smell faintly of smoke, topped with maple syrup laced with yogurt—smooth, creamy, and sweet against the coarse texture of the fragrant grain.

In the ashram, we went to dietary extremes. We moved from vegetarianism to veganism (no meat, dairy, or animal products). But that wasn't good enough. We decided to eat only raw food. We became borderline fruitarians, living on grains, fruits, and nuts.

Our diet expressed our commitment to Ahimsa, a concept central to Jainism, a religion in India that predates Hinduism. Ahimsa means "to hurt no one." Jain monks wear scarves over their mouths to keep from accidentally inhaling insects. They strain their water so they don't inadvertently swallow gnats. They let mosquitoes suck their blood.

Like the Jains, we in the ashram wanted a nonviolent life. We kept our own apiary and made our own honey. Why? In spring the hive grows crowded and creates new queens. The new queens leave the hive and the bees swarm, leaving with her. To ensure the original hive's continuity, beekeepers kill the new queens. What violence, we thought. How terrible! We wanted to make absolutely sure we consumed nonviolent honey.

Eventually I became disillusioned with Ahimsa. I had taken an orange in hand one day and was peeling it, but stopped halfway through and just stared at it for a while. Fruits, nuts, and grains we considered nonviolent foods. In other words, the exchange of energy from plant to animal is nonviolent, versus pulling up plants by their roots or killing an animal for its flesh. But the orange seemed to look back at me and say, What do you think the farmer did to make sure you got this orange? Herbicides, fungicides, insecticides, eradication of voles. I sat in horror. The list was endless. What about transporting the orange? The construction of roadways, the filling in of wetlands, the decimation of woodlands? What about the truck, the fuel, the insects slamming into the windshield? *Okay! Okay!* I thought. *I get the message.*

I had to question the kind of spirituality that I practiced in the ashram, a holier-than-thou posture that said to the rest of the world, I am above you! I am purer than you with my nonviolent honey and these full lotus asanas that are wrecking my knees. I realized that it was egotistical to think that we're above killing. We take life with practically every breath, each time we eat or drive a car. Our life is death.

It's important to recognize and acknowledge those deaths—to be aware, sensitive, conscious of the life we're taking so that we may live. Then we must live life to the fullest to honor these deaths. When we cry, cry. When we celebrate, celebrate. Don't waste life, either your own or all the beings that have died so that you can live.

———

THE DANCE OF LIFE AND DEATH

———

I dress in pants, jacket, and a wool parka, all colored with tree bark camouflage, multiple shades of gray with off-white streaks. The faint musky animal smell that adheres deep in wool's resins is released as my body heats, mingling with my human scent. I wear two pairs of socks, a fast drying undersock that wicks moisture away from my skin and a thick wool outer sock. I scan the contents of my pack: compass, tape measures, note pads for recording data, a clipboard and pencil, a thermos of hot cider, some food, an emergency kit, maps of the Quabbin area, knife, plastic bags for collecting samples, a camera and small tripod, several rolls of film, a caliper for measuring scat, field glasses, a flashlight, and matches in a waterproof compartment. I strap a rolled up length of closed-cell foam sleeping pad to the outside of my pack, to be used for sitting down where it's cold, snowy, or wet.

Paulette is up, puttering about. "Dress warm, Hon," she says. I hear in her voice and see in her face all her warmth and sweetness. Kissing her good-bye, I'm conscious, as always, that this may be the last time I'll see her. In my biker days, I almost died from motorcycle crashes. I've been confronted by cops with revolvers drawn, ready to blow my brains out. Since those days, death has been close and it's stayed with me. I can feel my mortality, the border between life and death, which is infinitely fragile, easily breached.

This is one of the lessons that tracking has taught me. The more intimate I become with nature, the more I am aware of the presence of death. We push that awareness back in our minds until it recedes. But death surrounds us everywhere we go. Each breath—meditating, tracking through the woods, sitting at my desk—is one breath closer to death.

Before leaving the house, I call the Metropolitan District Police to tell them I'm going into Quabbin's Prescott Peninsula. I talk to Jim, a dispatcher with whom I've spoken many times before. I'll be out of the area by dusk, I tell him.

"It's a cold one," he says. "Give us a call when you get home so we don't come looking for you."

"Right," I say.

And I'm out the door.

Prescott Peninsula is off-limits to the public. I drive through its gates, down a plowed road that ends in front of an observatory the University of Massachusetts has built far from any source of human light. The observatory's squat brick building is crowned with a large metal dome that houses a powerful telescope.

I'm enthralled by the news of space exploration, but I'm just as fascinated by what's close at hand. I notice, for example, tracks of a white-footed mouse moving laterally around the observatory's edge and then into the woods. I study the minute variations in the mouse's gait. Why do the tracks vary slightly here, lilting to the left? I look closely. The track patterns change, revealing the mouse's behavior. It's standing, huddled against the wall, whiskers quivering, plush velveteen nose sniffing the air, heart pumping fast. That mouse is breathing light from the sun. Its energy is the light of the sun. The same is true for me as I straighten, walk back to the Jeep, and flip open its hold.

I strap on large Alaskan snowshoes, shaped like fat teardrops with curved wooden frames. The snowshoes are old-fashioned, rather clumsy in dense forest. But I like their aesthetic, and I'm used to them. I've fitted them out with crampons, which keep me from slipping on the uphills.

Quabbin's population of forty to sixty deer per square mile creates a plethora of runs that crisscross through the woods, narrow passages etched in the snow. Runs connect bedding and feeding areas of the deer's range that is only about two square miles for each animal. I soon find fresh movement in a run that veers west. As always, when I find a fresh set of tracks, I'm filled with a sense of adventure. I'm going to go wherever this deer takes me today. I don't know where that will be or what I'll learn. I'm simply giving my life over to the deer and its destination.

I'm in mixed hardwood and hemlock forest. Deer have been moving through this area to feed, but in winter they prefer the shallower snow depths and shelter of heavy conifers to move through, rest, or sleep. Winter foods cannot sustain the deer. They live off fat reserves and try to retain their energy. For bedding areas they prefer a south-facing slope that's heavily wooded. A conifer grove on a knoll is an especially choice spot. You can see their beds, indentations in the foliage or snow, marked with bits of fur. Sometimes they'll sleep in groups, facing away from each other—sentries on guard against a predator's approach.

I follow the run, meticulously recording data. The whole forest is heavily browsed. Witch hazel, viburnum, hemlock, red maple, ash, and oak are so heavily impacted that the trees aren't regenerating. I'm careful to find and record only the freshest bite marks along the run that indicate what my deer ate. I can tell the freshly browsed twigs from the old ones. The green cambium layer under the outer bark browns within a matter of hours.

Deer urine stains the snow. It has fallen behind the hind tracks, revealing the deer's female sex. I watch for small changes in track patterns, for clues to what she's eating and where to look for her browse. Her tracks alternate, a pair on the left, a pair to the right, until she reaches for food, which is indicated by a track to the side that has not received her full weight. I notice different ages of scat along the run. The fresh scat of deer on winter forage are peanut-sized pellet groups, black to dark brown, glistening with a fresh mucus coating and very little smell. You start to see wood fibers in the pellets as scat dries.

The run takes me down a short steep slope. The snow has blown and piled against the shallow bluff, and the tracks penetrate the drifts a good eighteen inches. I empathize with the deer, negotiating the tricky winter terrain. If fat reserves become really low, the deer's bones may become weakened. It's not uncommon for them to break legs as they step through, or slip and slide on, ice-crusted snow.

The slope levels off, and I come to a small stream, gray humps of boulders showing through the snow cover. The sound of water is muffled, a deep, muted gurgle under an icy caul. I've hit a tributary of Thurston Brook and I follow it into a lowland expanse of white pine and hemlock. This is the kind of place in which I'd like to get lost come summer.

It's fairly flat, the trees well spaced, the browse line (the height to which the deer have nibbled away branches) is high, giving the woods an open, park-like feel. It's a place to walk quietly, sheltered from the wind, breathing in the piney scents of tar and sap that waft up from the soft needle floor. Conifers always draw me in. I want to enter them, losing myself with nothing particular in mind. Places in the forest beckon to me, and I follow their pull. It's something I do by myself.

The doe takes me into the conifers, where canine tracks veer into the run from the north. The tracks are oval, their gait linear. I suspect coyote. The tracks of a domestic dog are rounder and the gait sloppier. The tracks are too large for a fox, and my guess is confirmed when I see scat seven-eighths of an inch in diameter, smack in the middle of the trail, tight coils shot through with fur. With no wolves in the area, only coyotes leave this kind of sign.

I've been aware all day of how cold it is. The wind surges from the north through a clear blue sky and bites into my exposed skin. The pine canopy whooshes. Bare bones of winter branches rattle in the gusts. But as I start to track deer and coyote, I am no longer conscious of how cold it is. The animals take over.

Quabbin's deer and coyote relationships are reminiscent of the plains of East Africa where predator and prey move together. Lions loll in grass while zebras graze nearby, apparently unafraid. Quabbin tells a similar story. When deer can see coyotes, they are alert but often exhibit very little fear. I often find tracks of the two animals in plain sight of each other. The deer allows the coyote close proximity without a confrontation. I've seen coyote tracks come right up to deer and almost playfully dart back and forth, while the deer holds its ground.

Unlike dogs, coyotes almost never chase deer for long periods. Dogs will chase deer for miles. But coyotes look for opportunities. They often won't chase deer at all, instead visually inspecting and testing them for weakness. I've seen tracks where a coyote comes up to a deer, the deer bounds away, and the coyote walks off in the opposite direction.

It's lunchtime. I unlace my snowshoes and place my foam pad so I can sit with my face to the sun and my back against a large rock. I fish in my pack for my thermos of hot cider, happily munching a cheese sandwich and a piece of chocolate cake. Out of the wind, with the sun warming my cheeks, it almost feels like spring. The stream I've been following reminds me of a section of Fever Brook in the east section of Quabbin, only about three miles away through the woods and across the water. Fever Brook empties into a wetland where great blue herons roost. The herons have built chunky nests on the crowns of snags.

Early last summer, Paulette and I came to this pond to photograph the parent herons and their hungry young chicks. We left the house long before dawn. We wanted to get into position while it was still dark so we wouldn't disturb the birds. With a head lantern, I set up a camera with a 600 mm lens on a tripod. Then we hunkered down, hidden in the sedge, and waited for dawn.

It was a special time with Paulette. We were absolutely silent, deep in the woods, waiting in the dark for the light to come. When it came, blazing in the east, the herons started their day. We photographed the adults regurgitating food to hungry chicks—large ungainly birds, not yet able to fly—who looked like they were ready at any instant to topple from their precariously balanced nests.

The chicks went into an uproar each time the adults appeared, madly croaking and ravenously bopping up and down with gaping beaks. Those nests were bulging at their seams. Like their parents', the young herons' feathers were smoky blue and their profile pick-shaped, their long handle-like necks topped with flat skulls and sharp attenuated beaks.

Around noon we heard a splashing on the shore. Something big was moving, parting the grass, and coming toward us. Through the sedge, the sleek form of an otter appeared, nose in the air, fixing us with glassy, inquisitive eyes. After a brief inspection, the otter turned, slipping back through the grass. There was a small splash as it reentered the water.

Case closed, we assumed. But several minutes later, we heard splashing again. We looked at each other. *No way,* we thought. The otter was back, its fur dripping with water. Its eyes were black marbles and its whiskers were outrageously long. Pausing often, it came to within six feet of Paulette's foot. It just stood there, looking at us. Then, in silence, it bounded off, the muscular tube of its body sledding through the grass. This time there was a big splash, and Paulette and I began laughing.

With my belly full, it's hard to resist the temptation to lie back and bask in the sun. But I get up, roll my foam pad into a tight cylinder, refit my snowshoe bindings, adjust my pack straps, and retrace the latticed teardrops of my tracks to the run.

The snowshoes make a satisfying hollow flopping noise as I pad along on top of the snowpack. I'm far from the observatory road. My deer browses hemlock, reaching up into the trees, occasionally standing on its hind legs to clip a bough. A pale white sheen covers the sky like a blister. I'm glad that I ate lunch when I did. Now the sun is distant, riding low, almost on its way out.

For the last several hundred yards my deer has been behaving strangely. One or the other of its front hooves keeps moving off-kilter, to the right or left in the snow. I know this indicates that the deer tried to smell or nibble something, but the vegetation is untouched. It's a puzzle. I can see the deer, leg bent, carrying weight on its opposite foot, hind leg brought forward for support, long neck extended. But toward what? Finally, it dawns on me that the leaning prints occur whenever lichens appear trail-side. Is the deer smelling the lichen but not eating it? Is she eating something else near the lichen that I've failed to notice?

I traverse a south-facing slope exposed to the sun. The hardwoods are open here, growing straight and tall. I can see rust-colored tips on their high branches that in eight weeks' time will swell to buds. The snow is shallow on the slope, beaten back by the sun, and my doe has dug through it into the ground to find ferns, clipping off their tops, which are like little bundled knots ready to burst open in spring.

It's late afternoon, and the sun is now obscured by a haze of clouds. The wind gusts from the northwest, lowering the temperature to the teens, perhaps even colder. It's time to return to my Jeep. A compass bearing sets me off in a northeasterly direction. Forty minutes later, I pick up the observatory road. It feels good to be out of the woods, back on packed snow, reentering the human fold and its comforts.

Fresh tracks to my left head east into the woods. I check my watch. It's close to four. There's only an hour of light left. Not sure why, I start tracking. I move quickly as the temperature drops, ice forming on my beard and mustache. The woods are a mix of white pine, hemlock, and hardwoods—maple, oak, beech, and ash.

I snowshoe for a mile or more, drawn into the woods. I'm not sure what it is that makes me stop as I cross an old logging road. A knowledge that is pre-knowledge, visceral and in the cells? We wake from a deep sleep and turn off the alarm just before it rings. How do we know the moment has arrived?

Off to my left, I see a coyote and deer facing each other. They stand motionless on the edge of the conifers where shadows start. I want to lift my binoculars to see closer. But I can't move quickly. I'm surprised the animals didn't see me coming. They must have been so attentive to each other, their vision so tightly focused, that they missed my approach.

The only way to get my binoculars up is to move with excruciating slowness, a fraction of an inch at a time. If I move really slowly, the animals will not detect movement. It takes me several minutes to raise my field glasses to my eyes. Now I can see the animals clearly. The coyote is silver-colored, which is very rare (usually coyotes' coats are tawny). It's a magnificent animal, muscular, with a thick glistening winter coat. Its guard hairs bristle, gleaming in the last light.

There's blood on the ground.

The deer and the coyote stand perfectly still. The light is going, and my field glasses are wavering in my tired hands. Then, without warning, the coyote bursts toward the deer, and the deer, equally fast, lashes out with its hooves. I'm not breathing as the coyote retreats, circling. The deer whirls, and then the two animals whirl together. Snow flies as they spin—coyote lunging, deer pivoting. Suddenly, the coyote stops. It walks away slowly, not even looking back. The deer is perfectly still. I'm wondering: Did the coyote smell me? Did it see me? Why did it abruptly stop, then leave?

The deer stands frozen. My arms are exhausted from holding the field glasses to my face. My fingers are freezing. The cold is penetrating, sinking in, working its way toward my core. And now it's dusk. Jim and Paulette will be wondering where I am, but I don't dare move. I feel I have become part of the deer and the coyote's drama.

The deer begins to limp with what seems to be incredible pain. I can't believe it—it starts to browse! Now I can see clearly that its left hind leg is broken. The leg dangles uselessly. Bone cuts through the hide about twelve inches above the hoof. The deer moves awkwardly. My initial guess is that it has broken its leg during its confrontation with the coyote (later I learn that it had probably broken its leg in the snow). The one thing I know for sure is that the injury is fatal. And as I'm thinking this, I catch the coyote in the corner of my eye, slinking belly down in the snow toward the deer.

The coyote dashes and the deer wheels, lashing out again with its hooves. The animals fight this second time in a stand of white pines. Deadwood breaks. I can hear it cracking. Snow flies. Now I know what's happening. The coyote isn't taking any chances. It isn't wasting energy. The coyote knows the deer is in trouble. It's testing the deer, wearing it down. Time is on the coyote's side.

The deer whirls with balance and poise that would be astounding under any circumstances, but is miraculous given its crippled state. For a full five minutes the dance goes on. Then the coyote stops and walks away as if nothing has happened.

I'm shivering. My fingers are numb. It's dark and there are no stars in the sky. I realize I'm on the verge of hypothermia, and I need to move soon to get my blood circulating before it's too late. When hypothermia sets in, you become disoriented, start shaking uncontrollably, and lose your strength. I've been there before, and I don't want it to happen again, especially on Prescott, as night descends.

The deer limps into the deadwood. The coyote is nowhere in sight, but I know for sure he is nearby. Rubbing my hands together to keep warm, I leave this scene and head straight for my Jeep.

I know what I'll find when I return to the spot at sunrise the following morning. The deer is down. It's in the snow. A red-tailed hawk stabs at the carcass and takes flight when I get near. I don't approach things like this right away. I don't rush toward them. I always wait, stand still, take my lesson from the coyote. I'm very slow and cautious.

I think this type of approach applies in traumatic situations. When there's a crisis, a death, something that startles us, we often feel we have to act immediately and decisively. In fact, it's important to stop, pay attention, watch what's happening. It's key to monitor your emotions, the chemical responses in your body. What's responding is your past, your conditioning, and those responses are sometimes inappropriate.

When I'm certain there are no animals around the kill site, I move in. The deer is one hundred feet from where I saw it last. The coyote had started tearing into it from the rear, feasting on the deer's meaty hind quarters. The coyote had also ripped open the deer's belly. There, in the snow, still attached by an umbilical cord to its mother, is a fetus.

The fetus has spindly legs, a fragile rib cage, white hooves the size and shape of thimbles. Its body has no skin, just muscle tissue webbed with veins. I check the doe's leg. The hide and bone are worn away. The leg had been broken for some time, the injury probably caused by the doe crashing through crusted snow. It's early February and there is no way that she would have made it through the winter. The silver coyote that tracked her late one bitterly cold winter afternoon was a blessing in disguise.

I figure the coyote is close by, laid up, waiting to digest and come back to continue feasting. Fishers, bobcats, ravens, crows, snowshoe hares, chickadees, and weasels will all feed on the doe's carcass. Birds will build their nests from its hair. Head, skull, spinal column, bones of the lower legs—everything will eventually be carried off and eaten. The doe and its fawn are the coyote's pups and the hawk circling above.

I often think of the title of the book by Stephen Levine, *Who Dies?* Who indeed? When you think of the human body as a system, cells are constantly dying and being born. Yet we think of ourselves as living. We don't say part of us is dead and part is alive. On the other hand, the whole biosphere is a living system. But we say parts of it are dead and parts are alive. That's not the way it is. It's a system in flux, just like the human body, renewing itself constantly.

In his notebooks, Krishnamurti writes, "There is no creation if death does not sweep away all the things the brain has put together to safeguard the self-centered existence. . . . Death was the means to a new state, new invention, to a new way of life, to a new thought."

We can easily see that the death of the doe and her fawn can give birth to new forms of life. But it is not as easy to see that the death of an idea, especially one in which we find security, can give birth to something new. This something new is the unknown, as death is the unknown.

Self is an idea. It is all we think we have, so we hold on to it tenaciously. The self fights for its life in the same way as the doe. It has all the same survival mechanisms. It clings to its life, fearing death, fearing the unknown. But as Krishnamurti reiterated throughout his life, this is a posture of rigidity and stagnation. One must die to the self in every moment. Then every moment is fresh and new.

Standing over the doe and her fetus in the snow that chilly winter morning, it became clear to me that in every moment inside us the dance goes on, the dance of life and death as we die and are reborn. The dance of the self struggles to sustain itself. Its wall of resistance closes the door to something larger, more inclusive: our limitless potential, our original condition of oneness with each other and creation.

The hawk cries overhead and I see doe and coyote whirling in the deadwood at dusk. I see the coyote's silver coat gleaming in the last light, disappearing into the shadows of the hemlock and white pine, and then blending into the snow as it returns, without me, for its final charge.

The dance of life and death happens around us and inside us at every moment, in our own bodies and in every part of the universe. Our life and death are part of that dance. They *are* that dance. I find it good practice to acknowledge this, just as it is good practice to affirm life by acknowledging the value of important things. There are rituals and reminders that help us to live in reverence to the circle of life.

For example, if I appreciate someone in my life and inwardly take some time to acknowledge the person, that act strengthens my appreciation and makes it more valuable. But it would be much better if I told the person of my appreciation. How about giving her a gift? Now I have brought awareness to the value of the relationship and thus deepened it.

Sometimes it's important to express in a visible way what is meaningful. In some religions and cultures people bow to each other to acknowledge their connectedness. This makes the invisible visible. Native Americans give thanks in their rituals and ceremonies to the Creator for all life's gifts. Christians say grace, acknowledging the source of food, before eating. At Zen Buddhist monasteries, there are many rituals to acknowledge all the beings that have died so we can live.

So much in our lives is invisible. Take a phone call, for example, or the electricity coming into our homes. I lived in my home for over fifteen years without electricity. When the poles finally came down the road a few years ago, a strip of woodlands two miles along the side of the road was cleared. Paulette cried when she realized what was going to happen. It may sound ridiculous, but we both went to talk to the trees and plants, sometimes bowing to help express our appreciation for the sacrifice.

Of course, it wasn't just our two miles of road where that sacrifice had occurred. There are millions of miles of roads. Every time you go to make a phone call, stop for a minute. Visualize the invisible. Acknowledge the millions of beings who have died and who are dying so that you can make that call. Before you turn on a light switch or get in a car, stop, really stop, and take a moment to reflect on the invisible elements in each action you take.

Imagine that it's night and you're flying in an airplane above New York City or San Francisco. Imagine you're looking out the window, down on the glowing city with its millions and millions of lights, its beehive of activity, its hustle-bustle of consumption. For every ounce of consumption there is an ounce of death. Take responsibility for the whole city and bow to the beings who died so that the hive can live. Embrace the magnitude of it.

When you sit down for a meal, really look at what it is that you're eating. Acknowledge what that food is, where it comes from. I learned this lesson deep in the inner dunes of Cape Cod on a mid-August day. It was dry and hot, and I was carrying about thirty-five pounds of photography equipment, working on assignment, photographing the Cape's secret places for *Yankee* magazine. The temperature in the sun was close to one hundred, and the heat was reflecting off the sand. I'd drunk about half my water and the day was not half over, so I was trying to conserve the supply.

The dunes are huge, some of the biggest on the East Coast. In the low areas you can find natural cranberry bogs with highbush blueberries growing in them. The bog is ringed with twisted pitch pine growing to about ten feet. At the edges of the bog are lush patches of blueberry bushes, brimming with fruit at the peak of ripeness. I put my pack and tripod in the shade of the pines, planning to stay a while. There are many more berries here than I could possibly pick or eat. They are all shades of blue, ranging from periwinkle to dusky purple.

The bog is a small oasis, a hidden world within a world. It is very still and quiet, set in a basin surrounded by the high sandy dunes with their sparse covering of grass. The dunes stand like sentinels against sound and wind. People crowd the beaches a mile away, but the dunes keep the bog and its bounty hidden and secret. The bog has the feel of ancient wilderness, and I am completely alone.

I don't just gobble up the blueberries. First I look at them, plump and full of juice. I do this very consciously and purposefully. I look at the leaves collecting sunlight. The twigs are green, but as they get thicker in diameter, the bark turns a grayish white. I follow the trunks to the bog's sandy soil and layers of decaying plants. The bog is acidic and decomposition is very slow. I picture the roots sinking into the earth, gathering nutrients and moisture wherever they can. Tracing a line with my eyes, in my mind I follow the minerals, moisture, and organics back up through the roots, up the trunks and out to the leaves and berries.

I collect a handful of these succulent berries. They are surprisingly cool to the touch. I hold up the fruit to the sun and think: these berries are the sun, the moisture in the clouds and the air. I bring my hand with the berries low to the ground, close to the sandy soil. These berries are the sand of the dunes, the decomposition in the bog.

The sun sizzles on the sand. Light reflects in platinum sheets off the puddles of the bog and glints off the mosaic of the blueberries' green leaves. My thirst knows no bounds. Thousands and thousands of blueberries stretch before me, bursting with sweetness and juice. I put the handful of berries in my mouth, and the whole universe enters me: dunes, earth, light, and water. Life takes life. It is a sacred process. It is the doe hobbling through the cold, her leg dangling useless. It is the silver coyote slinking through the hemlocks at night for its final charge. It is the universe entering the universe. It is who we are: energy dying, energy living.

9.

COYOTE

INTELLIGENCE

I was walking in Green Mountain National Forest in Vermont, picking my way along a dry streambed. It was late August, a warm, clear day with hardly any wind. Animals have a hard time picking up scent when the air is dry, and my scent was contained by the ravine through which the stream ran. Only my head was visible above the stream banks.

I scanned the forest for wildlife. Movement in my periphery caused me to slowly turn my head. I was startled to see a coyote staring back at me. It soon moved off, and I thought I heard coyote yips, but I wasn't absolutely sure. Then I saw another coyote, moving along the same path as the first. It stopped, seemed to look back in my direction, and continued on.

I became very still. Two other coyotes appeared. They had more rust in their coats than the first two animals. These last two animals approached each other and met behind a tree. I was intensely curious to see what they were up to, but I didn't dare move and give away my presence. In a couple of minutes, the rust-colored coyotes moved out from behind the tree and stopped one hundred and fifty feet away from me at a deer carcass.

As the coyotes noshed on the carcass, I raised my binoculars. With the binoculars I could literally stare into their eyes, slanted and colored a striking bright yellow. Those eyes seemed to look past me and through me as if I wasn't there. Yet, for some reason I couldn't fathom, and which raised the hairs on the back of my neck, their attention was drawn in my direction. They would eat, stop, and stare toward me.

I didn't dare move. I felt as though I was going deep into those eyes, deep into coyote, into wildness, a place that has no abode, no face, and harbors no distinctions.

I had been watching these animals for a good five minutes when I began to feel surrounded by coyotes. Dark shapes moved deep in the forest. Now and then I thought I heard yips. The two rust-colored coyotes moved off the deer carcass. Another coyote came to take their place. I realized that I was witnessing a pecking order at the carcass: two older animals had eaten first, followed by two younger animals, perhaps siblings. Then a last coyote, possibly an orbit animal, had taken its turn.

I decided to try to shoot some photos, and ducked down behind the banks of the ravine. You shouldn't be able to sneak up on a coyote, but I thought I'd give it a try. I moved as quietly as I could, keeping trees between us, covering perhaps twenty-five feet in ten minutes. When I gauged that I was within photo range, I peeked around a tree. I was amazed to see the coyote was still there, and I figured that I'd get only one shot. I was one hundred and twenty-five feet from this animal, which, I assumed, would bolt when it heard the camera's shutter click. I took a photo. The coyote's ears perked up. It stared straight at me. Then it dipped its head back to the deer carcass, long snout pecking, salvaging the tiniest scraps. I took more photos, and each time the shutter clicked the coyote looked up. Eventually, it grabbed a bone and dashed off into the forest.

I checked the carcass. The rib cage looked like the skeleton of a wrecked ship: the long chunky twist of the spinal column; the skull in the shape of an iron, oddly flat on top. There was hair everywhere but almost all the meat had been scavenged. Maybe that's why the coyotes didn't stay long. There wasn't much left to eat. I watched the carcass for a while longer, but the coyotes did not reappear. I put my camera away and hiked back down the streambed.

Since that day, when I close my eyes I can see the pupils of the two rust-colored coyotes. There was something secret there, a wildness that didn't only belong to the coyote but that I recognized as my fundamental nature. It was who I was but it didn't belong to me. It was the intelligence of all beings. It was uncultivated, unbiased, and unconditioned. It was true intelligence.

Most of us equate intelligence with the thought process, the ability to gather, store, manipulate, and regurgitate information. Since animals don't seem to have that capacity (or, if they do, like chimpanzees, they have it to a lesser degree than we do), we tend to think of animals as unintelligent, or that their intelligence is narrow in scope. We think that animal behavior is governed by instinct, whereas our behavior, if we're acting intelligently, is determined to a large degree by thought. Our rational capacity gives us freedom to choose one course of action over another. Our superior intellect enables us to project ourselves into the future, anticipate the consequences of our actions, and learn from our past. We consider these capabilities indicators that our intellect elevates us above the animal realm of instinctual behavior.

To me, intelligence is not merely thought. By thought, I mean our inner dialogue, the process in our brain that figures things out, the many ways that we manipulate stored information. Our ability to think has been a source of pride for us since we first developed our own sentience. We call ourselves Homo sapiens, the thinking man. It is probably the primary way in which we define ourselves.

Thought is a very limited mechanism, although it does not think of itself in this way. Thought likes to think it is autonomous, instead of what it is—conditioned and reflexive. It is important to understand that, compared to intelligence, thought is severely limited. In *Wholeness and the Implicate Order,* David Bohm explores the limitations of thought:

> It is clear that thought . . . is basically mechanical in its order of operation. Either it is a repetition of some previously existent structure drawn from memory, or else it is some combination arrangement and organization of these memories into further structures of ideas and concepts, categories, etc. These combinations may possess a certain kind of novelty resulting from the fortuitous interplay of elements of memory, but it is clear that such novelty is still essentially mechanical (like the new combinations appearing in a kaleidoscope).
>
> There is in this mechanical process no inherent reason why the thoughts that arise should be relevant or fitting to the actual situation that evokes them. The perception of whether or not any particular thoughts are relevant or fitting requires the operation of an energy that is not mechanical, an energy that we shall call intelligence.

As Bohm points out, thought is based on the past. It's the movement of a bunch of accumulated images, responding to the dynamic present. Thought judges the present from past experiences. It is limited to the past and its conditioning. Thought can't move out of the past, get free of itself. It always looks with old eyes. Thought is a vehicle with tunnel vision.

The universe is one undivided movement. In that movement we perceive change because we are able to remember and store information of previous moments or events. Music has meaning because we are able to remember prior notes. There is meaning to these pages because we are able to remember previous words. Prior events stored in memory and in association with the changing moment give us the information with which we create our reality. Within this context, we have a sense of becoming. But this perceived reality is dependent on the mechanics of memory, bound by the past. To move beyond those constraints, we need to have the perspective of what I'm calling intelligence. Memory perceives things as changing and becoming, but intelligence is not affected by memory or becoming. Intelligence never changes because it is completely empty, silent, still, unmoved. It is not of time, not in time. It is not affected by time. It looks at the movement of becoming but remains unaffected or unbiased by that movement.

There is another fundamental problem in looking at the nature of thought in relation to intelligence. Bohm points out that thought is always mechanical and conditioned. Thought creates the thinker of the thought and that which is being thought—a dichotomy. This dichotomy divides us from intelligence. I have inherited the notion that I am the thinker of the thought. I am not going to let anyone tell me that *my* thoughts make me up, and that my idea of who I am is getting in the way of some great intelligence out there somewhere. Besides, I believe that almost everybody thinks this way. When I was in my mid-twenties, if someone had tried to convince me that *my* thoughts made *me* up, I would have probably suggested that he see a shrink. But after a few decades of self-inquiry, it's sometimes other people who look at me as if I should see a shrink.

There is an exercise you can do that might help you picture how this dichotomy that exists within all of us, and separates us from intelligence, was created. Visualize yourself as a mirror. This mirror is intelligence. It stretches endlessly into a void. There is nothing in front of the mirror, so it is reflecting nothing. You don't know you're the mirror, and since there is absolutely nothing in it, you don't realize you exist.

Suddenly, things start to appear in the mirror. These things are thoughts. You still don't realize you are the mirror, but you are clearly aware of the thoughts because the mirror is reflecting them. Then one of these thoughts says, "All these thoughts are *my* thoughts. *I* am aware of them and *I* am thinking them. *I* have control over them." This thought has separated itself from the rest of the thoughts and from intelligence. It has created an island called self. This self thinks it is intelligence, but it is really a thought.

The island of self is the thinker of the thought. The thinker is thought watching itself: the past is watching the past, the old judging the old. Not only is thought perpetually stuck in the past, it has separated itself from intelligence so it can't fully see itself. It can't be fully aware of its movement. It can't move in a fully rational manner, although it thinks it does. Only the mirror (intelligence) can reflect all its movements. The thinker of the thought doesn't know about the mirror. There is no way that the thinker can see it.

Bohm discusses this particular limitation of thought as a lack of proprioception, or self-perception. To illustrate this handicap of thought, he uses the example of a woman who wakes in the middle of the night, repeatedly hitting herself. "A stroke had damaged her sensory nerves," Bohm writes, "which would tell her what she was doing. But the stroke left the motor nerves so that she could still move her muscles. Apparently she had touched herself, but since she wasn't being informed that it was her own touch she assumed right away that it was an attack by somebody else. The more she defended the worse the attack got. When the light was turned on, proprioception was reestablished because she could see with her own eyes what she was doing, so she stopped hitting herself."

Neurobiology teaches us that thought is a physical process like any other physical process in our bodies. The electrical impulses animating our brains are tangible, concrete movements, what Bohm calls a "muscular reflex," often (though not always) far subtler than our typical knee-jerk reactions. Bohm urges us to be aware and attentive to the movement of thought, in essence to give thought self-perception, thereby linking it to what we are calling intelligence.

I began to grapple with the nature of thought when I started tracking the self at age twenty-seven. Tracking the self was a daily process of trying to be aware of the slightest, most subtle signs of thought. I found self wherever I looked, under every rock, behind every tree. I found out that thought had given birth to self. Self was an idea that said, These are *my* thoughts.

But self is just another thought albeit one that sees itself as real. Self grows constantly. It is a very arrogant beast, and it has turned things upside down. Self sincerely believes that it is the creator of thought when, in fact, it is thought that has created self. And in this case, thought is working counter to intelligence.

In my own life, this insight about the relationship between thought and self brought me to an astounding discovery: the belief that self is something real is at the crux of the whole human dilemma and all the unnecessary suffering we have created—all the pain of our crippling psychological fears, our inability to love one another, the hurt we inflict, our crushing sense of isolation.

Even though I was becoming intimate with the beast of self, there was nothing taking its place. I had discovered the falseness of self, but as self dissolved, I was left empty. It became clear to me that in my own life, thought was tracking thought. This was a torturous realization, a period of time that I likened to a desert—bleak, empty, and remorseless. Wherever I looked was emptiness. There was no water to quench the insatiable thirst of self to *become* something—in this case, not the leader of a notorious motorcycle gang but a spiritual, enlightened, realized human being.

I wondered whether I would ever emerge from this desert. Try as I might, I couldn't get away from thought. I was a dog chasing its own tail. Every time I thought I was on to something (Now I'm really doing it!), whenever I thought that I had grabbed on to self or had its trails all mapped out, I would realize that I had caught hold of my own tail again and find myself back in my own tracks. What I was seeing in myself was strictly mechanical and limited: thought and more thought. I began questioning: Are we, as human beings, products of our genetics, environment, conditioning, culture, and history? Are we unconscious and mechanical beings? Are we, at least potentially, free, conscious, and intelligent? I knew that my perspective of thought was limited—no matter how facile or embracing—because thought inevitably abstracts, limits, and defines. The present is never truly contained in thought: analysis cannot cover the moment of analysis. I clearly saw thought's inability to fully observe its movement from the perspective of itself.

I knew that thought alone could never know the full meaning of coyote, stone, and wind. It could never sink its roots into the soil like the oak or smell the soil as its own flesh. It could never taste its own blood in the mountain stream or soar on the wind. It could never know true humility, spirituality, love, compassion, truth, awareness, or wildness. I learned that to truly know these things requires an intelligence that is free of the past and independent of thought. I learned that this intelligence permeates everything, and everything is contained in it.

It's difficult to talk about an intelligence that permeates everything or is aware of everything, because intelligence cannot be quantified or measured. Think of intelligence as a box. Sensory perception and thought are simply the contents of this box. The contents have a certain "intelligence" of their own, but it is limited. When thought examines thought and content examines content, we are inescapably stuck in this box, because thought breeds thought. When thought tries to free itself, it just creates more content.

It's common for me to see my tracking students working inside this box. Thought would like us to think that it has all the answers and is the only tool available to us to understand our world. This is the model that thought foists upon us. We expend a tremendous amount of intellectual energy attempting to figure out *why*, the reasons for the way things are. When my students ask Why? I tell them to wait and watch and observe. I tell them to pay attention and remain open to what the forest is showing them. Once, a group of tracking students and I walked along the shore of Tully Lake. We came to some new tracks in the sand under tall drooping dry grass that glowed golden in the late summer sun.

"What are these?" I asked my students.

I made myself comfortable, squatting on my heels. I hoped there were no experienced trackers in the group because I didn't want the answer to come too quickly. There was a good lesson here. The tracks were half circles, about twelve inches long. They were made of fine lines, as if someone had taken an uneven two-inch whisk broom and gently rubbed the sand with it. The tracks were certainly not left by an animal's foot. So what had left them?

My students' intellects immediately seized the question. Thought was like a Harley, taking off in a drag race, rubber burning. There was smoke everywhere!

Answers came swift and fast. The students had very capable intellects.

"A fox's tail, whooshing back and forth in the sand," one suggested.

"No," another countered. "The fox would have left tracks, and there aren't any."

"A bird swooping down after insects left wing marks," said a third.

"No, I think it's probably made from the tail feathers."

"The marks are at least an eighth of an inch deep. It must be a big bird, like a hawk, after a mouse. There are mouse tracks only a couple of feet away."

"That cinches it. It must be a hawk's wing marks."

"No, tail feather marks."

They were all very pleased that they had come up with such an ingenious explanation for the mystery tracks. Thought was doing its thing. It had found the answer. They turned to me for confirmation, and I shook my head.

"No," I said, "not a small bird, fox, or hawk. Try leaving your brains out of it. Your intellects are creating too much smoke and clouding the issue. Try silence, try observation. Let the answer come to you instead of trying to make it happen. Just sit and look at the tracks. They may have something to say. But in order to hear, you must be quiet. Thought must be still."

A few people sat down and the rest stood around. We all stared, waiting for the tracks to speak. Several minutes passed before a light breeze blew in.

"Look! Look!" a student noticed. "The grass is moving in the wind. The drooping blades are making marks as the wind blows them back and forth!"

"So," I said. "Now you see. When your mind is still, you can track the wind."

We think that if we dissect the past and apply all our reasoning powers to the subtle nuances of cause and effect we will come to understanding. If only it were so. I am not saying this is wasted energy. But inside the box our thinking and movement are nothing but a sophisticated form of knee-jerk reactions. This we mistake for intelligence.

Outside the box is freedom from the shackles of time, an opportunity to see in a radically new and fresh way. True intelligence—an intelligence that is boundless and free, no longer constrained by thought, no longer *self*-contained—shatters the box. When we discover this true intelligence, we discover a universe ripe with the possibility of change. Leaving the box, we realize that we can make a difference, because we don't live in a predetermined, mechanical universe. The universe is limitless. Things can change despite the past. Our lives have meaning, and what we do with our lives matters.

10.

THE
WILD WITHIN

WILDNESS IS NOT SO FAR AWAY. SOMETIMES IT IS MUCH
closer than we think. I remember once approaching the frozen shores
of Somerset Reservoir in Vermont and glancing out over an expanse
of ice. A quarter of a mile away, six coyotes disappeared single-file
into the forest. I thought, *How amazing that there are so many coyotes
around.* Some biologists think there are more coyotes than foxes in
North America. Yet we hardly ever see coyotes, even though their
wildness is among us. It is everywhere, but it is hidden and secret.
Most of us don't know much about the world of coyotes, but coyotes
know a lot about ours. They watch and listen to us.

One winter day I tracked a fisher with eight students. The fisher
led us up the north slope of Bemis Hill to a small bowl cut into the
hillside. It was a hard spot to get to. Below the bowl was a cliff, above
it a steep slope, and to either side thick stands of conifers. Inside the
bowl were ten coyote beds in the snow, small round circular indentations where the animals had bedded down. Some of the beds were
quite close to the cliff's edge. From their vantage in the bowl, the coyotes had a good view of the Millers River and the railroad tracks below. The hillside was cupped like an amphitheater. Every sound that

came up the slope was amplified. The coyotes couldn't have picked a more strategic position. The location was unapproachable without their notice. I stood in the bowl, astounded that I could see and hear every sound down in the valley where I live. The coyotes must have been aware of my every movement. Although we are often unaware of wildness, wildness is aware of us. It is everywhere.

Through tracking we can find coyote fortresses, learn the language of the forest, and become intimate with an animal's life. But how do we come to know our own true nature? How do we find the metaphoric coyotes inside us, which are watching and listening to us but of which we are mostly unaware? How do we live the wild within?

One of the ways I have suggested in this book is to practice tracking the self. But this practice can sometimes become a trap. It can work against the awareness that is the wild within. I can't tell you what your own path will be. I can only show mine in hopes that it will help you discover your own entrapments. My practice, my journey inward, was fraught with entanglements, distractions, and wanderings, which, in the end, were valuable lessons.

Practice was what my life in the ashram was about. I adhered to a strict diet of raw food, spent countless hours in sitting meditation, and practiced hatha yoga with complete and utter devotion. Looking back on those days, I have to smile at my dedication. When I first started doing yoga in 1971, I couldn't bend over with my legs straight from a standing position and touch my toes. I was as stiff as a stilt.

But it's amazing what practice will do. I started off with a daily twenty-minute yoga routine. Two years later I was doing a minimum of two hours of yoga each day. *Light on Yoga,* by B. K. S. Iyengar, was my bible. My routine consisted of a twenty-minute headstand, standing postures, forward bends, postures to strengthen my abdominal muscles, hand balances, back bends, and twists. I finished with a sitting meditation that lasted from ten minutes to one hour.

At the height of my yoga practice there weren't many postures that I couldn't do. My transformation from stilt-man to pretzel-man convinced me that with hard work and perseverance I could master anything. I still think this is true. With practice, we can all become expert trackers, doctors, lawyers, writers, or painters. Whatever we want to do with our lives, we can. There are going to be limits, but we should be able to overcome most of them.

But there are limits to practice in the spiritual realm. Practice means to repeat in order to master or strengthen. Practice is cultivation and organization. But how do you practice something that can not be cultivated or organized, and is unrepeatable? How can you practice the wild within? Spiritual practice is different from practicing to become a skilled tracker, engineer, lawyer, writer, or artist. Spiritual practice is about *un*becoming.

One of the best ways to understand the spiritual practice of unbecoming was the story I told you earlier of the young monk who was told by his master to meditate but not to think of gorillas. The young monk's practice was a magnifying glass on his inability to control his mind. The intention of the practice initiated by the master was to maximize the limitations of self, to make the hidden more obvious.

During the young monk's meditation, thought was trying to control thought, self trying to control self. Self needs to see that it is not in control. The truth was staring him in the face but he couldn't see it. The awareness that is wildness was there in the wings, waiting for the slightest weakening in self's pride. Seeing—awareness—had to enter while self still had the illusion of being in control. Seeing had to be in the moment and not an afterthought. When seeing is an afterthought, seeing is the seeing of self taking credit for seeing its own limitations. Self takes a hit, but then immediately takes credit, reestablishing its pride and sense of control.

In some ironic way, practice helped to demonstrate to the young monk that practice could not silence the mind. Practice was shouting louder and louder, "I can't do it! I can't do it!" But the young monk was avoiding the truth, saying, "I can do it. I am doing it." At some point, the young monk needed to realize and accept the truth that not only was self not in control, but it was actually in the way of a greater awareness. Only when self becomes tired and weak and pride languishes can the awareness that is wildness step in.

With my practice, I eventually came to the same place as the young monk. On the one hand, I saw the futility of practice. On the other hand, I realized that it may be important for most of us, myself included, to practice and study intensely. I learned that it's crucial that we be clear about our practice. Why are we doing it? Too often, practice is a trap. The self begins to believe that it is wildness. We need to constantly question our practice. Is it teaching us about ourselves? If not, then we need to change our practice. Is our practice making us uncomfortable, irritating and humbling us? Then our practice is working. Spiritual practice is a paradox. It won't create seeing, but it will set the stage for us to see what seeing is not.

It was during the years in the ashram, living a very disciplined and intense practice, that I realized my true nature was wildness. Eight people lived in a seven-room house. The core group came together because of our interest in self-inquiry and yoga. We studied Krishnamurti and any other literature we could get our hands on that explored who we are, the inner structure of our thoughts and feelings, and our relationship to a greater whole. I had become certified to teach all levels of hatha yoga by the Sadhana Yoga Centers of New England, and I was training most of the core group to be yoga teachers.

During the period when we had the ashram, people would come and go, but usually there were around seven of us, including my wife and two children. Gabriel and Corinne were the first to join. I had met them just after my gang days, and they quickly became good friends. I connected with Gabe immediately. He was a charismatic storyteller and a deep, sensitive man. Corinne was a true flower child, gentle and ethereal with long, flowing dresses and tresses. Art, a handsome man in his early twenties, joined us soon after we started the ashram. He, too, had aspirations of being a yoga teacher.

The ashram's first floor had been made into a large open classroom that could hold about thirty students. We opened another yoga center in downtown Providence, Rhode Island, and called these centers Jnana yoga communities. Most classes involved teaching yoga, but we also offered classes in satsang. The word *satsang* is from the Sanskrit *sat,* meaning truth, and *sang,* meaning association.

To give satsang means to sit and talk with people or to give a talk about truth. Satsang classes are verbal inquiries into truth about who we are, our notions of self. Satsang was what I understood Krishnamurti to be doing when he talked and lectured around the world.

I dubbed myself a Hatha Jnana Yogi. One of the advertising posters for my classes read, "Can you be your own guru? Jnana Yogi Paul Rezendes invites you to find out for yourself." Krishnamurti repudiated gurus and authority figures of all types and insisted that the means to self-realization are available to all of us, independent of any teacher or religion, if we pay attention and honestly and rigorously look inside ourselves. Jnana yoga is in this mold. It teaches that truth or consciousness cannot be cultivated. In its deepest form, Jnana yoga says that we are never separate from God, or the whole. Our true nature is already oneness. So any act of seeking oneness is a denial of oneness.

Jhana yoga seemed to fit with Krishnamurti's philosophy and life, which were really what we were following, although that went unsaid, because Krishnamurti did not accept any followers. In fact, Krishnamurti said over and over again that he was not a guru, not a teacher. He repeatedly stressed that if you wanted to find truth, you could not follow anyone. You had to find it yourself. So although Krishnamurti was our teacher, he wasn't. We couldn't acknowledge him as our teacher or leader. It was against our unspoken rules. Yet we all acted like little walking and talking Krishnamurtis. Imitating him, we didn't have any leaders in the ashram. I was, however, permitted to have the title of director, and my wife, co-director, but any other form of leadership was not tolerated.

Krishnamurti said that we could not practice our way to truth, freedom, awareness, or love. But we knew that he did hatha yoga, sat in silence, and was a vegetarian. So we emulated him and sat in meditation, did hatha yoga, and were vegetarians. We did all this for health reasons, since we weren't supposed to be doing it to find truth or become enlightened. That was also against the unspoken, supposedly nonexistent rules.

As Krishnamurti had done in his talks and writing, in our interactions with each other we went right for the jugular of self. If one of us looked like he or she was becoming attached to some practice or any kind of effort to become spiritual, become compassionate, become this, become that, someone inevitably pointed out that whatever it was he or she was trying to accomplish was ego driven. If one of us claimed to be practicing compassion, another would point out that if compassion was part of our daily life, then he or she wouldn't be seeking it through practice. We put our emphasis into seeing that we didn't have compassion or awareness. Our energy went into seeing what compassion and awareness were not, rather than seeking them.

We pointed out each others' limitations. Sometimes this was constructive and sometimes it was simply one-upmanship. Once I was criticized for how I walked down the stairs. A student said to me that anyone who walked down the stairs with such heavy footfalls had to have ego problems. Much to my amazement, he was serious.

We relentlessly tracked down the self. We were merciless. You almost wanted to feel sorry for the self with no place left to hide, nothing left to hold on to. The cunning, conniving animal of self was running for its life. But from whom? Who was this relentless tracker? Was it wildness, the one who leaves no tracks? Not always.

I came to see that some of my self-inquiry was phony. Self was afraid, hiding under its cloak of self-observation. As long as it could see itself involved in self-observation, it had the illusion that it was capable of tracking itself, that it was the tracker. My self-observation had an ulterior motive: under the guise of seeking the truth about itself, self was really interested in its own development and growth. Self wanted to become wise and spiritual. It wanted to capture truth and hold it and examine it and experience it. It wanted to be a truth-seeker and a truth-sayer. It wanted to feel beautiful, powerful, and pure. Ambition had clouded the truth about its limitations. Fortunately, despite all this confusion and veiled egoism, there was a quality of energy that cared more about truth than about self. That energy was wildness, waiting at the door that the self had kept closed so that self could not see its limitations and helplessness. The image that self held of itself as the tracker was its closed door.

During this period I was trying with all my might to follow Krishnamurti's dictum, "Pay attention." This was supremely important to Krishnamurti. During a talk he gave in Saanen, Switzerland, on August 3, 1969, recorded in his book *The Flight of the Eagle*, he said:

So my concern is to be aware of inattention. What does that mean? Because if I try to practice attention, it becomes mechanical, stupid, there is no meaning to it; but if I become attentive, or aware of lack of attention, then I begin to find out how attention comes into being. Why am I inattentive to other people's feelings, to the way I talk, the way I eat, to what people say and do? By understanding the negative state I shall come to the positive, which is attention. So I am examining, trying to understand how this inattention comes into being.

This is a very serious question because the whole world is burning. If I am part of that world and that world is me, I must put an end to the fire. So we are stranded with this problem. Because it is lack of attention that has brought about all this chaos in the world. One sees the curious fact that inattention is negation—lack of attention, lack of "being there" at the moment. How is it possible to be so completely aware of inattention that it becomes attention? How am I to become completely, instantly, aware of this cruelty in me, with great energy, so that there is no friction, no contradiction, so that it is complete, whole? How do I bring this about? We said it is possible only when there is complete attention;

*and that complete attention does not exist because our life is spent
wasting energy in inattention.*

That's what I thought I was doing: constantly trying to watch myself,
whether I was teaching hatha yoga, meditating, talking to someone,
hoeing the garden, tending my beehives, walking in the forest. But
this was not observation from the perspective of wildness. It was self
observing self, thought observing thought. I was practicing my idea
of awareness. The awareness I practiced was not the awareness that is
wildness. It was cultivated, just another neat little row in the garden
of self. The door was not yet open, wildness was still not real. The
only thing happening was that thought was doing its best to mimic
wildness.

It was in this period, during a walk in the forest, that I discovered
who was tracking self and much, much more. One day, when I
needed some time alone, I walked behind the ashram's large organic
garden and beehives into a swamp of small shrubs and red maples.
This swamp backed up to a hillside of tall white pines. The pine forest had a luxurious carpet of needles, marvelous stuff to walk on. The
warm weather had just arrived, and the sky was a magical blue.

While walking I watched the movement of thought, conscious of
every step and aware of the light, airy feeling of my body from yoga
practice, meditation, and the raw-food diet. The air was thick with
early summer smells and white pine pollen, which was so copious
that it painted the forest floor a subtle yellow-green. My footfalls sent
delicate pollen wisps swirling around my feet, turning my white
sneakers a psychedelic chartreuse.

There was no hurry. I was just there, being me, having spent
about six years of intense inquiry into truth that began when I saw

the young Mama being abused. I started questioning who I was and whether my life had meaning. This self-inquiry deepened and took on a new urgency when I came close to being gunned down by the police and narrowly escaped prison. These events forced me to examine my life, which had to be more than just the pursuit of pleasure and the avoidance of pain. I had had my fill of pleasure. I had wallowed in sex and drugs and personal power. Yet somehow I could never fill the cup of desire. It was always half empty.

After my bust, I decided that the answer to the questions that I was asking about the nature of self and the meaning of life must lie with God. I naturally turned to my roots in Catholicism, the faith of my parents. If I became a good Catholic and went to church, took the sacraments, and led a pure Christian life, I thought I would come to know who I was and life would have meaning. But there was a big problem.

I could not become a full, practicing Catholic because I was married to a woman who was still married to her first husband in the eyes of the Church, which didn't recognize her divorce. I was living in sin. In order for me to be fully accepted into the Church and to be able to take the sacraments, my wife needed to get an annulment of her first marriage. The only other option, if I wanted to pursue Catholicism, was to leave my wife. I opted for an annulment.

My wife and I wrote to the Pope, asking for the annulment. I took a vow of celibacy and prayed and prayed, crawling on my knees through the stations of the cross at La Salette Shrine and Seminary in Attleboro, Massachusetts. I talked to Christian monks and studied St. John of the Cross. I did this with total abandon, believing I was asking for the right thing. After all, I reasoned, it wouldn't be right for me to forsake my wife and children. All I wanted was to be a good Catholic.

I did all of this for a whole year. The celibacy part was one of the hardest things I have ever done. When the Pope's answer came, it was an unequivocal *no,* which shook me to my core. I really believed that God would answer my prayers, because I sincerely believed that I was asking only for what was right. It seemed to me that my prayers not only went unanswered, but that no one was listening. I had to admit that I didn't know if there really was a God. For once in my life I didn't care about pain or pleasure, my image of myself, or my need to belong. I just wanted to know the truth. What was life about? Was there a God? Who was I? Was life just about the pursuit of pleasure and pain, or was there some greater meaning? I began to realize with an undeniable clarity that my pursuit of God and spirituality was no different than my pursuit of pleasure. It was all in the name of self-gratification.

I didn't realize it at the time, but a new energy had entered my life. It was the awareness that is wildness, and it wouldn't accept anything but the truth. And it was this quest for truth that led me into this beautiful forest of white pine, walking along on a warm day in early spring, admiring my psychedelic sneakers, and doing a good job, I thought, of observing myself and paying attention as Krishnamurti had exhorted all of us to do.

Then the extraordinary happened. Suddenly there was a "seeing," an awareness that the awareness I had been practicing was blind. Self was watching self, thought was watching thought. Self could not see its whole movement, but, at the same time, there was a "seeing" of the whole movement of self. This "seeing," though, did not come from self. Thought didn't make this one up. It was like coming upon a bear in the forest. There was no denying it. Something was showing me that I couldn't see. My blindness was revealed to me despite myself. Wildness was revealed.

In that moment I saw that wildness was the whole universe. All things were manifesting in it. Wildness was the bear in the Adirondacks, the coyote and the doe in their dance of life and death. It was as if I had been asleep all my life and had been dreaming about being a gang leader and a yoga teacher in an ashram. I had woken up and realized that I was not just the gang leader, yoga teacher, thinker of the thought—I was the universe, every rock, tree, cloud, animal, and person on the planet. I was the moon and stars, intelligence, awareness, compassion, love, direct communication, the dance of life and death, and the web of life. A door had opened, and the wild blew in.

I was floored. The thinker of the thought was totally inept. This is what I, the self as the thinker of thought, had been avoiding. I had avoided seeing my limitations. The self that thought had created was incapable of awareness. But by practicing phony awareness, I had been able to maintain the illusion of achieving awareness. I saw that, ironically, my practice had helped bolt shut the door to wildness, to awareness, to the master tracker, which is what all of us are in this conscious state.

As I walked back to the ashram I thought about what a paradox my enlightening experience was. My true nature was wildness, but I was still Paul Rezendes. My practice was the closed door to wildness, but how could I have seen the folly of my practice if I wasn't doing it? I realized that, although in one sense the earth had moved for me and the most significant event of my life had occurred, nothing had happened. Everything had changed, yet nothing had changed. Zen Buddhists have a saying that expresses this paradox of enlightenment:

Before enlightenment the valleys were valleys and the mountains were mountains. After enlightenment, the valleys are valleys and the mountains are mountains.

This saying expresses the awareness carried out of the woods with me that day. Over the years, I used the following interpretation, called the Mountain and the Valley, which I gave to my meditation students and now give to my tracking students, to explain the paradox of existing as the whole universe and yet remaining an individual.

Before enlightenment, the mountain and valley were always in conflict, always afraid of each other. The mountain felt the valley was encroaching on it, taking over its territory. And the valley felt the same way. The mountain was encroaching on it, threatening its very existence. The mountain and the valley were always at war. Until they realized, Hey! Wait a minute! There is no mountain without a valley nor valley without a mountain. There can be no back without a front or front without a back. Each supports the other. The essence of each is intrinsic in the other. They realized that their true nature was not separate, and they were dependent on each other. At the same time they both realized, AHH, yes! I must be fully the mountain, different from the valley. And, yes! I must be a valley as best as I can be a valley. In being a valley, I support the mountain. And in being a mountain, I support the valley. But even with this sense of their individual identity they realized that their true nature was one. They kept their identities, but their identities did not rule them or fragment them. Instead, their identities took their proper places, a small portion of who they were, a smidgen of their larger wholeness.

The Mountain and the Valley is instructive because it illuminates the fundamental nature of reality. Although the mountain and the valley appear separate, they're inseparable. They are one. Zen Buddhists have a gesture called *Gassho,* putting their two hands together, palm to palm, and bowing. The two hands represent the mountain and the valley, their separateness, the left and right, good and evil, the pirate and the girl, day and night, the doe and the coyote, life and death. Bringing hands together symbolizes the fact that all seeming dichotomies and dualities are one. Bowing recognizes and expresses gratitude to that fundamental nature of oneness. To me, that oneness is the wild within, although in reality, it's as much out there in the universe as it is within us.

We all have moments when we are absolutely present, alive, and awake. But what does it mean on a daily basis to live the wild within? For me it means to live fearlessly. To have no abode, because every place is home. To have no face, because you wear every face. To be nothing because you are everything. To have no path because you walk all paths and know that every path is the wrong path and the right path at the same time. It means to have no religion because you accept and have compassion for all religions. It means to have no color and to be brown, white, black, and yellow all at the same time. Perhaps, most of all, it means to be humble—to have a sense of humor about yourself and your life.

A few days after the walk in the woods when I had had my enlightening experience, a thought occurred to me. Does this moment of insight mean that I'm enlightened? The next instant I burst into uncontrollable laughter, as if I'd just heard the funniest joke in my entire life. Tears gushed from my eyes so profusely that I couldn't see. This was unfortunate because I was driving a tractor-trailer truck on a crowded New Jersey highway with no shoulder. I had no choice, however, but to stop. I was laughing hysterically, far too deeply to drive. I stopped the semi right there on the highway, off to the side. Holding my gut, flattened across the steering wheel, I could not stop laughing. Cars and trucks whizzed by. It's a good thing no state trooper stopped to check me out, because I don't think I would have been able to stop laughing. It could have been quite a scene. "Officer, I'm sorry. I just found out I'm not enlightened!" I could picture myself saying that, and then roaring with hysterical laughter.

After about fifteen minutes convulsed over the steering wheel, weak from paroxysms of glee, I calmed down enough to get the semi going. I took the first exit off the highway, still laughing. I don't think I ever laughed so hard or so long and with so much joy.

What hit me as so absurd was that it was the thinker of the thought that asked the question: "Does this mean I'm enlightened?" Poor egotistical self, it couldn't go to the party. It was incapable of seeing its dilemma, yet it wanted to know if it was enlightened. The self just wouldn't quit!

Self cannot take credit for enlightenment happening. The thinker cannot possess it, have it, claim it, or accomplish it. There is nobody there to pat on the back and say, "You did a good job, Paul." There is no reward because, in a certain way, there is no one who is able to receive anything. The thinker is unable to say, "I've arrived, I have it, I'm enlightened." The thinker has to take its place in a little corner of the universe, understanding its limitations. With this understanding, the thinker no longer divides thought. Thought is whole, no longer limited. Thought dances with wildness to write these words. But thought also interrupts the dance to say, "It's a beautiful spring day. I want to hike in the forest, track a bear, and photograph the landscape." Thoughts happen, as inevitable as the sun rising and setting. We can listen and observe, but no response is needed.

Self lives as a ghost in the temple of wildness. Life and death are not separate. The Dalai Lama, the Pope, the pirate, and the Devil's Disciples are my brothers. The snake, dove, porcupine, bear, sun, moon, and stars are my sisters.

Gassho.

Permissions

Grateful acknowledgement is given for permission to reprint from the following:

Commentaries on Living, 1st Series, p. 186, by J. Krishnamurti, edited by D. Rajagopal, ©1956 by Krishnamurti Writings, Inc., A Quest Book (1967 edition). All rights reserved. Used by permission of The Theosophical Publishing House.

Wholeness and the Implicate Order, pp. 50, 51, by David Bohm, ©1980 by David Bohm, ARK Paperbacks, an imprint of Routledge, London. All rights reserved. Used by permission of Routledge, London.

Thought as a System, p. 121, by David Bohm, ©1994 Sarah Bohm (first published in 1992 by David Bohm Seminars). All rights reserved. Used by permission of Routledge, London.

The Flight of the Eagle, p. 125, by J. Krishnamurti, ©1971, Krishnamurti Foundation, London. All rights reserved. Used with permission of HarperCollins, Inc.

For more information regarding Paul Rezendes'
nature programs please contact:

Paul Rezendes
3833 Bearsden Road
Royalston, MA 01368-9400
e-mail: reztrack@tiac.net
or visit our website at
www.mossbrook.com/rez/

ABOUT THE AUTHOR

Author of Tracking & the Art of Seeing, *Paul Rezendes teaches thousands of students through seminars and year-round outdoor workshops, and is an internationally published photographer whose work has appeared in calendars and publications, including* The New York Times Magazine. *Regularly commissioned as a wildlife consultant by conservation organizations, Rezendes lives in Athol, Massachusetts. His collaborator on this book, Kenneth Wapner, is an award-winning journalist and author of* Catskill Rambles. *A resident of Woodstock, New York, he develops book and film projects through his company, Peekamoose Productions.*

DATE DUE

JUL 27 '99	

DEMCO, INC. 38-2971